Making the Most of

CLEMATIS

Raymond J. Evison

This edition, fully revised, published 1995 by
Burall Floraprint Limited, Wisbech, UK

First published in the UK by Floraprint Limited, Nottingham
Copyright © Burall Floraprint Limited, 1987, 1991, 1995

A CIP catalogue record for this book is available from the British Library

ISBN 0 903001 69 1 (paperback edition)

Floraprint books are published by Burall Floraprint Limited, Wisbech, UK

Picture Credits
All photographs by the author or Burall Floraprint with the following exceptions:
Harry Smith Collection, pages 30, 52
Neil Campbell-Sharp, pages 36, 40, 58, 83
Garden Picture Library, pages 37, 41
John Elsley, pages 62, 63, 65, 66
John Fielding, page 64

Page 1 and chapter pages 'Anna Louise'

Edited and indexed by Jane Robinson
Typeset by Angela Dix
Line drawings by Alan Payne

Printed in Singapore

Foreword

Raymond Evison has been involved with the genus Clematis for over 35 years. During this time he has built up a collection of over 500 species and cultivars. In recent years, he has been fortunate enough to travel widely; his lecturing engagements have taken him as far afield as China, Japan, Poland, Latvia, Estonia, the United States and Canada, where he has had the opportunity of searching for clematis species and cultivars in nurseries, gardens and in the wild; his greatest love.

His nursery in Guernsey, is one of the largest clematis production nurseries in the world, producing clematis for the wholesale markets throughout the world. From there he has introduced many species and cultivars to provide gardeners worldwide with an ever-increasing choice of clematis.

In 1984 Raymond Evison founded the International Clematis Society and in 1989 became the Society's first President.

He has been much involved with the work of the National Council for the Conservation of Plants and Gardens and is also currently a member of Council of the Royal Horticultural Society. His knowledge of clematis is based on years of practical experience and is blended with a love of plants which must be obvious to all those who have attended his lectures.

Acknowledgments

The author would like to express his sincere thanks to Mary Shirville of the National Association of Flower Arrangements Societies for her helpful comments on the chapter 'Clematis as a Cut Flower'. He would also like to thank both John Elsley, Greenwood, South Carolina and Tom Hawkins, Florasource, California for their help and advice in the preparation of the chapter 'Growing Clematis in North America' and in particular to John Elsley for his advice in making the hardiness zone recommendations. Finally he would like to thank his editor, Jane Robinson, with whom he has had the pleasure of working again in the preparation of this third edition.

Clematis x durandii

Clematis viticella 'Sodertalje'

Clematis 'Niobe'

Contents

An Introduction to Clematis

The extent of the range of clematis available today—differing size and colour of flowers, flowering period, the type of growth, variations in foliage, etc.—gives the gardener a bewildering choice when selecting which species or cultivar to plant where and with what. But it does allow the imaginative gardener and plantsman an unlimited freedom of choice of planting site, colour combination and plant association. Creating a colour scheme with foliage and flower as if an artist: not with a brush, but with living plants; not on a canvas but in a garden! What could be more exciting or rewarding?

The genus clematis (yes, it is pronounced <u>klem</u>-a-tis) is a most rewarding and fascinating group of plants which varies enormously throughout the world in the shape and formation of flowers, leaves and leaflets.

Most of the species native to the northern hemisphere are deciduous, the exceptions being the evergreen Mediterranean C. *cirrhosa* and its forms, together with the Chinese evergreens such as *armandii*, *uncinata* and *meyeniana*. The southern hemisphere greatly extends the range of both deciduous and evergreen species. However, it is the charming New Zealand species, such as C. *australis*, *forsteri* and *paniculata* that are the most useful and attractive. Sadly, these are not entirely winter hardy in cold northern European or Northern American gardens, but they are most successful if grown in conservatories or garden rooms, adding colour and, in some cases, scent.

The flowers of the species vary dramatically in form and shape, from the nodding, pitcher-shaped flowers of the American clematis, through the small bell and star-shaped flowers of the European clematis, to the large flat erectly-held flowers of the species *patens* which hails from China and has naturalised in Japan. In addition to these there is the important and great wealth of species in all forms that are native to the Himalayan mountain range such as C. *montana* and C. *orientalis*, and the herbaceous or subshrub forms of clematis from China such as C. *heracleifolia* with its hyacinth-like flowers.

This great variation of the species extends to the cultivar and large-flowered clematis that have been produced during the last one hundred and sixty years of which many of these old clematis are still amongst the most popular cultivars of modern gardens. The first cultivar, C. *x eriostemon*, was raised in London in 1835 and was thought to be the result of a cross between C. *integrifolia* and C. *viticella*,

China, Japan and the Himalayas are home to a wealth of clematis species.

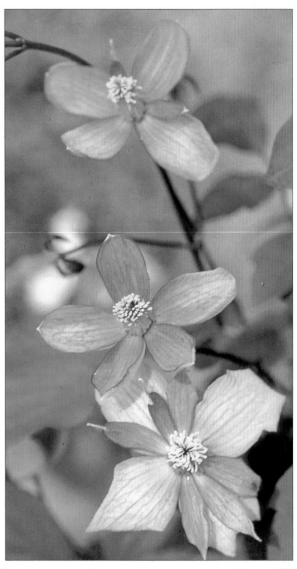

These two clematis are from Group One. Clematis montana 'Pink Perfection' on the left is easily recognisable and widely available. Clematis montana 'Broughton Star', right however is unusual but still most attractive.

both European species, the former being a herbaceous clematis. The resultant cultivar was a tall-growing non-clinging plant, still grown in present-day gardens.

For the more technically minded there are over three hundred clematis species distributed throughout the world. This book will be concerned mainly with the species and their cultivars which are native to the northern hemisphere, along with their cultivation and uses in a modern garden: whether it be formal, informal, patio or the natural woodland garden where the robust species clematis can be allowed to run riot, enjoying life to the full with the freedom to ramble and climb without restriction.

Regrettably, many of the three hundred species have no, or at least little garden value, and are of interest only to the clematis collector, botanist or hybridist. However, their presence has given rise to the very splendid cultivars of today.

Three main groups

The clematis of important garden value that are offered for sale and grown in their millions today may be divided into three main groups. The splitting and grouping is used purely for the convenience of cultivation, the ease of identifying the flowering habits, and most of all the pruning requirements.

Group One consists of the charming species and their cultivars which produce their main batch of flowers in early spring. The flowers are produced on short flower stalks directly from the leaf axil bud, generally on the previous season's ripened stems. This group has a range of species, in-

An Introduction to Clematis

cluding the evergreen forms and which flower first of all, the charming *alpina* and *macropetala* types flower next and our old reliable friend C. *montana* follows closely behind, although their rampaging nature is so unlike the more compact habit of the evergreen forms and the alpines.

Group Two cultivars also produce their flowers from stems which grew the previous year and became ripened before the autumn frosts. The ripened leaf axil buds produce strong new stems which may vary in length, depending upon the cultivar, from 10–30cm or even 60cm each, with a single large flower at the growing tip.

This group consists of the early large-flowered cultivars such as 'Nelly Moser' and 'The President', the strange doubles and semi-doubles such as 'Vyvyan Pennell', and the very large-flowered cultivars such as 'Marie Boisselot' which start flowering before mid summer.

Group Three clematis flower on new growth from mid summer onwards—all the previous season's stems become almost useless and die away naturally each autumn. This group of clematis are most useful garden plants and vary from the large open flowers of the *x jackmanii* types to the starry-shaped flowers of some of the European species to the dainty nodding flowers of the yellow C. *aethusifolia* from China. The interesting clematis of herbaceous habit also fit into this group, varying in flower and foliage from the delightful urn-shaped flowers of some of the North American species to the nodding European species of *integrifolia* and the hyacinth-like flowers of the *heracleifolia* types which are native to China and Japan.

Flower colours and form

The selection of flower form and flowering habit is indeed extensive and the variation in flower colour is quite fascinating. The delicate shades to choose from are mostly pastel colours,

These are two clematis from Group Two. 'Anna Louise' top, is an impressive new introduction while 'Elsa Späth' has been around a long time.

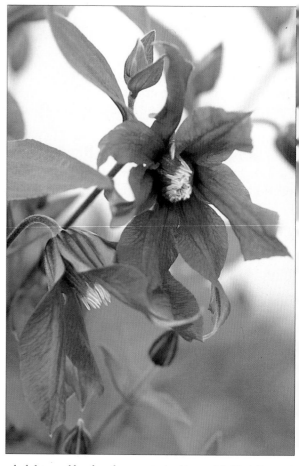

These are two clematis from Group Three. 'Madame Baron Veillard' on the left is an old and easily recognised cultivar, while 'Petit Faucon' is a stunning new cultivar.

not overpowering or too loud, allowing freedom of colour association with other plants and flowers. Purple, blue and mauve are the predominant colours, although regrettably the blue is not a clear blue as with a delphinium which is a close relative of the clematis, both being members of the Ranunculaceae family.

The reds also are not a pure colour since the nearest true red contains shades of blue or purple, but they blend perfectly with most garden planting schemes. The pinks are refreshing and are of various pastel shades, frequently having two tones, giving a bar or star-like appearance as with the ever popular 'Nelly Moser', whose blossoms are often described as resembling small cartwheels. Even the deepest shades of pink fade gently in

bright sunlight and are therefore not ideal for a sunny, south-facing position. This can, however, be used to advantage because the early-flowering pinks are ideal for brightening up a dull north-facing position where the sun's rays do not reach the freshly opened flowers, thus avoiding premature fading.

A large-flowered, deep buttercup yellow clematis is yet to be produced; and for the time being, the yellows are represented by the deep yellow, nodding flowers of *C. tibetana*. For the gardener with a little imagination, the creamy-yellow flowers of 'Guernsey Cream' and 'Wada's Primrose' are, of course, deep yellow! Both of these cultivars are most delightful and, if grown in a north, west or east-facing position will retain their creamy yel-

low colours better than if planted in full sunlight.

The white-flowered clematis are very elegant and some of my favourite clematis are amongst the whites. Many of the large-flowered cultivars have such a pure colouring, and the starry-flowered species look superb if allowed to grow through dark foliaged evergreens, such as hollies and pines. The colourful part of a clematis flower is not called a petal, as with most garden flowers, but a tepal. The petals are absent, except in the case of some of the *alpina* and *macropetala* clematis which have petaloid stamens. Many garden flowers such as the rose have green tepals and colourful petals, the tepals protecting and guarding the delicate petals as they form in the flower bud before the flower opens.

Greening of flowers

During a season when plants are late in producing their flowers due to bad weather conditions, some clematis flowers often open green, the correct colour appearing later as the flowers age and the tepals are subjected to the sun's rays. Often, if this occurs, the flowers do not completely attain the true colour, the centre of the tepal remaining slightly green. This is almost certain to occur with white, or very pale pink or pale blue cultivars.

The very early flowering cultivars of the early large-flowered section such as 'Edith' or 'Dawn' (Group Two) should be planted where they will receive some direct sunlight. They should not be planted in a cold north-facing position. The varieties susceptible to the unwanted greening of flowers are noted in the Glossary on pages 78 to 122 and are not recommended for a north-facing position. These green flowers are delightful if one is a keen flower arranger, or has a taste for the unusual. A plant of C. 'Moonlight' that I once grew through a *Garrya elliptica*, which was on a cold north-east facing position, always produced its first flowers during cold springs in a delicate shade of green. These never failed to arouse interest with visitors to my garden.

Scent

We are fortunate in having a small selection of clematis which gives a pleasant scent; regrettably, even with the wildest imagination and on the warmest spring evening, this perfume cannot be compared with that of a rose. The species *flammula*, which is a native of the northern Mediterranean shoreline, is perhaps the hardiest of the strong-scented clematis species that can be grown and flowered in northern British and European gardens. The hardiest of all the strong-scented species known to me must be the "Sweet Autumn Scented Clematis" grown widely in American gar-

If a clematis is late in producing its flowers because of bad weather conditions, the centre of the tepal becomes green, as this Clematis 'Guernsey Cream' shows.

dens. *C. terniflora* (my American friends still incorrectly call it C. *paniculata*) does not flower well for us in northern British and European gardens. Our summers are neither hot enough nor long enough for it to perform well.

The strongest scented clematis species that I have grown is one that I have known as a form of *C. forsteri*, a New Zealand species. Many of the species from New Zealand have hybridized in the wild and there is some confusion over their names. Recently, cultivars have also been produced in England. However, my C. *forsteri*, which needs to be grown in a conservatory or cold glasshouse, has the most delightful scent (that of lemon verbena perhaps). It is very free flowering and is a must for the conservatory.

Another strong-growing species with a good scent and white flowers that I have grown for a few years is C.

thunbergii from South Africa which flowers towards the autumn. It needs a very sheltered spot, as does the Tasmanian species C. *gentianoides* which flowers well with protection in the early spring. The European species, C. *integrifolia*, has forms that are scented. C. *integrifolia alba*, which I am growing for the first time, has a delightful, strong scent.

Another European species *recta*, a clematis of herbaceous habit, has a very sickly sweet scent which is so heavy it is nearly unpleasant. A delightful, pale pink *montana* cultivar called 'Elizabeth' has a most heavenly scent when in full flower at the end of April. On a warm evening one is sometimes tempted to linger in one's garden with the scent of 'Elizabeth' until the moon rises! However a fairly new introduction C. *montana* 'Mayleen' with pink rounded flowers is the strongest scented of all the montanas that I grow.

A few of the large-flowered clematis have a woody scent—that perhaps of violets—but one's imagination is most definitely needed with all of these, with the exception of 'Fair Rosamund'. Unfortunately her flowers are a washy pink or off-white, not the best of clematis from the point of view of flowering or long performance, but still worthy of garden space. The foliage of C. *heracleifolia davidiana* when it becomes dry during the early part of winter is very heavily scented and this is possibly the reason why the form was collected by the monk Abbé David such a long time ago.

Attachment of clematis to host plant

The genus clematis offers such a wide variety of flowering habit, size, shape and colour of bloom, even a selection of scented forms, that one wonders what other peculiarities can remain. As far as I am aware there is only one other, and that is the manner by which clematis attach themselves to their host. The clematis, unlike other natural climbers, does not attach itself by sucker pads as does a virginia creeper, or with aerial roots in the case of the ivy, and it does not strangle its host. It gently twists its leaf stalk (petiole) around the nearest support, securing itself against anything except the strongest of gales.

The gentle attachment of most species and cultivars is embarrassed only by the over-vigorous nature of the *montana* family, which if allowed to ramble up a wall on to a roof is quite likely to gently, but forcibly, remove any tiles as it searches for suitable supports and light. The weight of growth when an established *montana* is in full foliage has also been responsible for bringing down telephone wires—so be warned, keep your *montana* family under control!

Clematis 'Arctic Queen' is an outstanding new, fully double, clematis with a very strong habit.

An Introduction to Clematis

Site, Soil and Aspects of Planting

The planting position of a clematis in relationship to its host or support and the thorough preparation of the planting site are vitally important. Obviously, if the correct choice of clematis species or cultivar has been made, and it is then planted without thought or correct soil preparation, all will be lost; or, at best, life could be made extremely difficult for the unfortunate clematis. Plain common sense and a little gardening knowledge are all that is necessary. I do not intend to give strict instructions, but simply describe some of the pitfalls, and advise on the most successful methods I have found regarding soil requirements.

A clematis will undoubtedly be expected to grace its host or support for many years to come, barring accidents of course. So, if the reader spends even as much as one hour on the planting site, religiously carrying out the advice that I am about to give, if not insist upon, then that time is little in comparison with the many pleasurable years ahead.

I must be honest regarding one clematis that I planted (or rather did not plant) which now adorns a wall-trained shrub, *Garrya elliptica*, on a bone-dry strip of soil at the base of a cold east-facing wall. Through the *Garrya* grows *Clematis* 'Moonlight' most successfully. No thought or soil preparation took place: the clematis was simply placed under the shrub and inadvertently forgotten. When I finally remembered, the clematis had firmly rooted itself into the soil through the thin paper pot it had been grown in. I apologised and gave the plant two gallons of water and it has never looked back and has flowered well every year since.

Planting Position

When considering the planting position, it is wise to think and remember where the most successful clematis species grow in their wild habitat. The species produces many thousands of seeds annually, many germinate and start into life in various places—even in what may appear to be bone-dry cracks in a rock face. However, one dry summer and disaster strikes! The most successful seedlings establish themselves underneath the overhanging branches of a shrub or tree where their requirements will be satisfied. The host's branches will shade the clematis roots just below the soil surface, at the same time allowing sufficient rainfall to penetrate to the root system, and the clematis vines can attach themselves to the host plant. This simple lesson from nature, of where the clematis survives best in the wild, should be used as a guideline when planting in our modern gardens. In fact, very often when I have been looking for clematis species in the wild, especially in China and Japan, I have found clematis growing out from underneath rocks, stones and scree. Sometimes when I have traced the clematis plant's main stem to find its root system, it has been buried beneath as much as 60cm or more of stones and scree giving the plants plenty (!) of shade and, of course, moisture. I do not suggest that we should cover up our clematis plant's root system to that degree, but it is a point worth remembering.

No clematis in the wild would flourish or perhaps even survive if planted within a few centimetres of the base of a wall in a bone-dry strip of soil (unless the gardener has "green fingers" like mine!). Likewise, it would be difficult for a clematis to establish itself at the base of a tree with a large trunk which would be surrounded with again very dry soil. It is possible to establish a strong-growing clematis species in such a site, but it does take time, patience and lots of water. It would also be foolish to attempt to grow a clematis if its root system had to compete for every drop of moisture and natural food from the soil with the hungry feeder roots of a small tree or shrub. *Laburnum*, hawthorn and lilac can be perfect hosts but their hungry root systems have to be overcome by the correct

1. Strong cane leading shoots to wall or trunk
2. Soil level
3. Top of rootball at least 5cm below soil level
4. Mixture of loam, peat or peat substitute, and bonemeal
5. Main base roots slightly loosened
6. Garden compost or rotted manure
7. 45cm
8. Sides and base of hole broken up
9. Base of plant at least 35cm from base of wall
10. 45cm
11. Small plant to shade clematis roots
12. Additional support

Planting a clematis against a wall and a tree

1. Strong cane leading shoots to main framework of shrub or archway
2. Soil level
3. Top of rootball at least 5cm below soil level
4. Mixture of loam, peat or peat substitute, and bonemeal
5. Main base roots slightly loosened
6. Garden compost or rotted manure
7. 45cm
8. Sides and base of hole broken up
9. Base of plant at least 60cm from main stem of shrub
10. Base of plant at least 15cm from base of archway
11. 45cm
12. Small plant to shade clematis roots

Planting a clematis against a shrub and an archway

Clematis 'Hagley Hybrid' is a later flowering, large flowered hybrid.

planting position, soil preparation and sufficient watering after planting.

Soil Preparation

It is advisable on all but the most perfect soils to carry out some soil preparation before planting. The exact site has been chosen, now the hard work begins. A hole, to a depth of 45cm with a diameter also no less than 45cm, should be dug, removing the good topsoil and placing it in a different place from the subsoil from the base of the hole. The subsoil must be disposed of but the good topsoil can be used again when refilling the hole.

If the soil is a very heavy clay, and soil preparation takes place during wet weather conditions, the sides of the hole will compact and appear like an impenetrable concrete wall to the young feeder clematis roots. So, before replacing the fresh soil, the side and bottom of the hole must be broken up as it is vital that no firm flat surfaces are left surrounding the hole. If the base of the hole is also not broken up this may retain too much rainwater and the clematis roots will possibly spend part of each winter with very cold frozen roots, which may decay causing a great deal of damage.

Back to the important hole! Before it is refilled, two forkfuls of well rotted farmyard manure, or well decayed garden compost, if available, should be placed at the bottom of the hole and lightly forked in; this rich compost or manure must be kept away from the young clematis roots and placed only at the bottom of the hole. Mix two bucketfuls of peat or peat substitute and two handfuls of sterilized bonemeal with the retained topsoil and place into the hole and lightly firm using one's feet. If, when removing the soil from the planting site, the topsoil is found to be extremely poor then this can be replaced by using old John Innes potting soil, or a mixture of equal proportions of loam, peat, sand and grit. When planting on very heavy clay soil, or very porous sandy soil, additional peat or peat substitute may be used giving the newly planted clematis every chance of quick and safe establishment in its new site. When refilling the hole, replace with a little extra soil to allow for sinkage.

When to plant

The best months of the year for planting clematis previously established in a container are the spring months, late March until the end May, or the autumn months, end of August until mid-November when gardening in Central Europe but in warmer climates this will be somewhat earlier and in cold areas such as North America or Scandinavia where spring arrives later, planting will need to be delayed.

One must not rule out the remaining months. Clematis planted during mid-summer or mid-winter if the soil conditions are favourable, will establish satisfactorily, but require much more attention. Nearly all clematis plants supplied by nurserymen are grown in containers and therefore can be planted throughout the year without causing distress to the plant, as long as sufficient water is applied to the freshly planted clematis during very dry weather conditions.

If a clematis is planted during the early spring the plant will establish itself easily during what is the natural period of growth for a clematis but it is important that the plant receives sufficient water until it becomes established. It may take five or six weeks before the feeder roots have become rooted into the compost provided in the planting site. Until this time moisture can only be gained from the root ball that existed before planting and water supplied by the gardener. As with other plants, do not just water the area where the stem emerges from the soil, water the surrounding area to a diameter of at least 30cm as this will then encourage the roots to grow into

Planted with its roots in the shade Clematis texensis 'Pagoda' will flower from July to September.

the surrounding soil as they look for and find the moisture provided.

When planting clematis during the summer months, it is vital for the plant's survival that it receives at least one gallon (4.5 litres) of water per day during dry weather. The soil must be moist and stick to the fingers when touched. Check the soil 8cm from the surface. If only dusty soil remains on your fingers the clematis requires water, and this could be for a period of eight weeks until the root system becomes established into its new surroundings. It would be my advice that the planting of clematis in hot climates should not be attempted during the summer months.

If planting is carried out during the period between the early autumn, the safer and easier life becomes for the establishment of your clematis. Unless the summer has been especially dry, the soil should still hopefully be warm from the summer months and this will encourage quick root establishment. Clematis plants normally stop producing foliage from early autumn onwards until the next season but the root systems continue growing until the win-

ter becomes cold and the soil temperatures drop low.

During mild winters when conditions allow the gardener to cultivate the soil, clematis may also be planted. The plant will merely exist and not attempt to establish itself until the soil temperature rises and daylight hours increase. It is not advisable to plant evergreens, or the less vigorous species and cultivars during the winter months. Even species such as *alpina*, *montana* and *tangutica* quite often will fail if they have to exist for several months immediately after planting in very cold wet soils, particularly if the soil is naturally a heavy clay. This can happen even when thorough soil preparation has previously been carried out. However, planting under trees where the soil is drier during these winter months can be an advantage. The soil condition under trees during this period is generally not too wet and can be warmer than an open garden situation, so that the clematis can start into growth as soon as the temperature rises. Hopefully the plant can then be partly on its way towards establishment before the dry spring

Once the root system has been thoroughly soaked, place the rootball into a hole so that it is buried at least 5cm below soil level.

check this the leaf axil buds should be visible by this time and will give a guideline to the plant's health and possible performance during the following summer. The choice of plant should be one that has several strong swelling leaf axil buds at the base of the stem (not at the top). With the late-flowering species and cultivars, especially the *x jackmanii* group, the new growth will appear right at the base of the previous season's growth, or even from below the soil level in the container.

Planting a young clematis

Before removing the plant from its container, submerge it in a bucket of water for 15 to 20 minutes; this will soak the root system thoroughly and will help the plant until the roots start to take up moisture from the freshly prepared site.

With a trowel dig a hole in the soil large enough to take the root ball, allowing sufficient depth so that the root ball will be buried at least 5cm below soil level. This deeper planting will help in the event of damage during future cultivation or by animals. If damage at soil level should occur in the future the plant will produce new growth from below the soil level from dormant leaf axil buds; thus, in the event that the clematis stem should become severed, even on a mature plant, the plant will not be lost. This deeper planting will also help and is strongly recommended for another reason: if the clematis plant, at some stage, might suffer from 'clematis wilt', then the more deeply planted clematis will almost certainly grow again from below soil level. More can be found out about the clematis wilt problem on page 76 under Pests and Diseases.

The plant should be removed from its container after the root system has been soaked but do not submerge for longer than 15 to 20 minutes: plants, like humans, can have too much

and summer months when lots of water will be required to make the plant's life bearable until its roots are firmly growing into the new site. Under some overhanging evergreen trees this establishment could take eighteen months; but be patient, because it is worth the extra effort, and the reward will be yours when the clematis is in full flower.

Choice of plant

When purchasing a clematis from a nurseryman, or garden centre, it is not important that the plant should be the tallest, or the most costly. If the plant is in a pot no smaller than 9cm in diameter, growing on a cane 30–40cm high, is strong in appearance with healthy foliage and a thick stem at the base of the plant, then this type of plant will grow satisfactorily. The smaller plant will just take a little longer to gain maturity since one buys time when planting a larger plant.

For successful establishment it does not matter whether or not the plant is in flower when bought. If the clematis is purchased during the late summer months, or early autumn, the leaves may be starting to die off, because, remember, most clematis are deciduous. If a clematis is bought during the winter, old leaves may still be left on the plant and to all appearances the plant may look dead. To

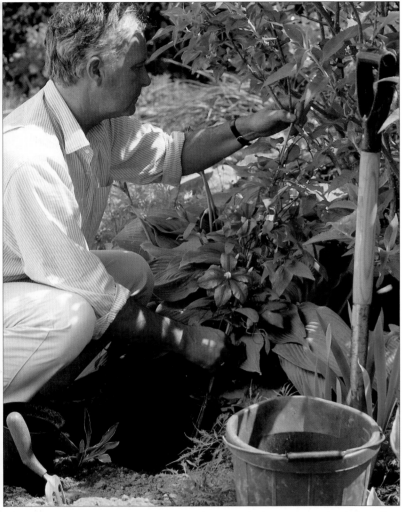

When the plant is at the correct depth secure a cane to the host plant to provide good support.

water! The bootlace-like roots of the large-flowered cultivars which are at the base of the container and probably growing in ringlets may be slightly loosened but do not disturb the main root ball as this will be fatal. However, if only a few roots are freed this will help the plant establish much more easily. On no account should the root systems of the fibrous-rooted species and their varieties be disturbed and great care must be taken with the root system when planting this type of clematis. The root systems of species such as *tangutica, orientalis,* the *alpina* types, *macropetala, C. potanini* var. 'Fargesii', *flammula, serratifolia* and *vitalba* are all quite distinctive from the large-flowered cultivars. They all have very fine, thread-like root systems when young plants, as compared with the thick bootlace-type of roots of the large-flowered cultivars. If in doubt, don't disturb the root system. The plant can be placed gently into the hole and firmed well by pressing the soil carefully, but firmly, around the root ball.

Initial training

The cane or support to which the clematis stem has been attached in the container must not be removed. Another cane should be placed near the root ball, secured to the existing one and then itself secured to the host plant or support. The main stem of the clematis must have a firm support, otherwise damage may occur through wind.

As the newly planted clematis produces new growth this should be carefully trained and tied into position on the supporting cane until the stems reach the support or the main framework of the host plant or tree. As a firm rule, all newly planted clematis should be pruned down to at least 30cm the first spring after planting. The exact time will depend upon location but it should be before bud break. This almost severe action will be rewarded by a more busy, compact clematis. It is important that a strong framework of lower stems is established and the young clematis must not be allowed to grow away producing only one or two stems. Admittedly, it is more difficult to achieve a bushy plant of the late-flowering, large-flowered cultivars due to their natural habit of growing from only just above ground level each year. However, hard pruning and pinching out of the young stems of the early-flowering clematis is rewarded in a bushy, compact plant, well furnished with flowers. Give up a few flowers the first year and hope to get double or treble the following years. Be an optimist, as I am with my clematis, and look forward to the future.

Moving an established plant

The replanting of an established garden clematis is always a challenge but with care and a bit of luck it may be achieved. The only time when success can reasonably be expected is during the months of very early spring before bud break when the plant is in its dormant period, or at least just coming out of dormancy.

If the correct pruning procedure has been carried out during the plant's lifetime, a large proportion of the top growth must be removed, ideally down to about 40–60cm. The stems must be cut just above a pair of strong leaf axil buds: do not cut into an old stem that shows no sign of life. Tie the remaining stems to a strong bamboo cane which should be placed firmly near the root crown but beware of new shoots which may be just under the surface of the soil as you will need every leaf axil bud and possible new growth points in the coming months.

Dig a circle around the root crown to spade depth and a diameter of 60cm with the root crown in the centre. Carefully lift the root ball out of the hole, with help from another person: do not be tempted to pull the root ball by the top growth, that would be fatal. Place the root ball onto a sack or polythene sheet, taking care to leave as much soil around the clematis root system as possible. The clematis may then be replanted into its new site, which should be prepared in the same manner as for the young clematis, but of course a larger hole needs to be prepared. The plant should be planted 5cm deeper than in its previous position. The first spring and summer after planting, the soil surrounding the plant must be kept moist at all times—plenty of water. The remaining top growth should be carefully tied into the support at its new site.

The large-flowered cultivars are the safest plants to re-establish, the fibrous-rooted species the most difficult as their very fine roots drop away as they are being moved and with very little root being retained re-establishment is generally not possible.

Annual feeding and mulching of established plants

For an established clematis which did not receive the ideal soil preparation, additional feed or enrichment of the soil is needed to prevent a slow decline of the plant. The ideal time for feeding clematis is during the very early spring months when the plant needs every bit of food and moisture it can obtain to produce strong healthy foliage and

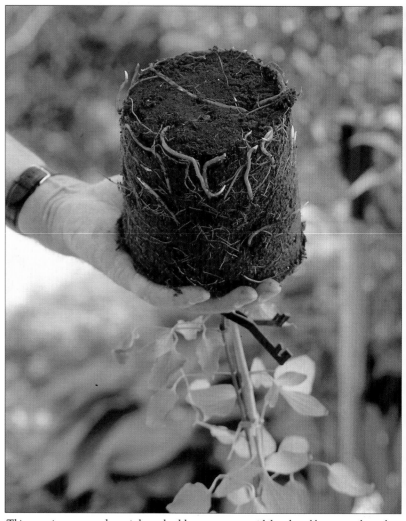

This container grown clematis has a healthy root system with bootlace-like roots—but when planting do not disturb the main rootball.

flowers.

Feeding can take various forms. If available in late winter or very early spring, well rotted farmyard manure or well rotted garden compost makes an ideal feeding mulch because not only does the mulch feed the clematis but, if spread thickly enough on the soil above the root system, it will give additional shade to the roots and also enrich the topsoil in the process as the manure decays. The mulch should be placed on the soil near to the main stem of the plant to a depth of 8cm and to a diameter of 50cm. Care must be taken not to place any of the rotted farmyard manure on the main stem or foliage of the plant as this will cause

damage. A space of at least 12cm around the stem must be left.

If rotted farmyard manure is not available, a mulch of peat or peat substitute placed in a similar manner will suffice. This should be mixed with sterilised bonemeal at the rate of two handfuls of bonemeal per two gallon bucket of peat. After the mulch has been placed on the soil surface it may be lightly forked in using a small hand fork. Care must be taken not to damage the feeder roots which will be very near to the soil surface. In the event of no rain within two weeks, the mulch should be moistened with at least two gallons of water which will stop the peat from blowing away and will also assist the bonemeal to enter the top-soil and reach the clematis feeder roots.

If mulching is not a practicality, the use of liquid feed is another alternative. There are numerous liquid feeds available and any of the well-known brand-named products can be relied upon. It is important, however, that the liquid feed chosen is a well balanced general feed. The liquid feed can be applied during watering during the spring and early summer months, as per the instructions on the container. If the soil where the clematis is growing is dust dry, the plant must receive at least two gallons of clear water before the liquid feed is applied. It is, however, important that feeding should be stopped just before flowering commences: that is, when flower buds on the most forward flowering stems are the size of a pea. If feeding were to continue during the build-up to full flowering and during flowering, then sadly the flowers would mature much faster, thus reducing the flowering period of the plant.

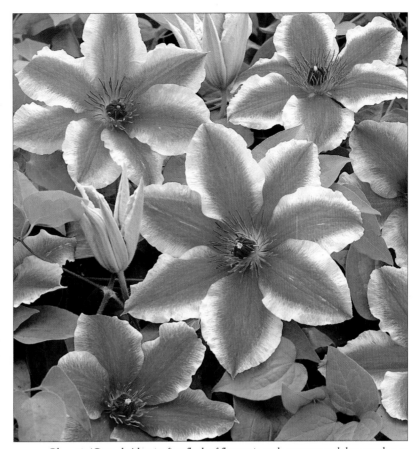

Clematis 'Carnaby' has its first flush of flowers in early summer and then another at the end of the summer.

Pruning Techniques

The pruning of clematis is probably the most talked about and written about aspect of clematis cultivation. What is a very basic and simple subject has regrettably been discussed and reviewed in such detail that the pruning of clematis has become unnecessarily complicated, causing confusion to both the experienced gardener and the newcomer to clematis growing.

Nurserymen in preparing their plant lists and catalogues (and I too have been guilty of this) have gone into great detail regarding pruning. Species and cultivars have been listed under different types of clematis, generally according to the large-flowered species from China and Japan (and their cultivated forms) such as *patens*, *florida* or *lanuginosa*. It is these and other species which have given rise to the hundreds of cultivars being produced before the early 1900s. The problems and details increased and became more entangled as new cultivars were produced and offered for sale. Therefore, with every good intention to help and assist their customers and readers, the nursery trade and writers of gardening periodicals have given rise to much unnecessary confusion regarding pruning.

As a gardener gains experience with growing clematis they will try to vary their pruning technique to suit an individual plant's own growth pattern which can change from year to year. Whatever they do, their aim will be to achieve the largest number of good quality flowers and healthy foliage.

After making the initial statement that pruning is a simple exercise, I have carried on to explain that pruning can then be varied from the basic technique as experience is gained; and it is at this point that confusion has occurred, with conflicting opinions being offered to the gardener. My intention, therefore, is to give the reader basic pruning requirements from the first spring after planting for each of the three different groups of clematis which were described on page 8. If you subsequently want to find out which type of basic pruning your own clematis should receive, look up the name of the plant in the Glossary on pages 78 to 122 and there you will find the pruning group specified.

If you are a beginner to clematis growing, the techniques illustrated on page 26 are entirely adequate and I suggest you delay reading my comments on more advanced pruning and training until you feel quite confident with the basic methods!

For the more experienced gardener the following detail may be of further guidance. You will have gathered that clematis either flower on previous seasons' ripened stems, or on stems produced during the current flowering season. The date when the clematis starts to flower is the all-important point and with this in mind pruning requirements become self-explanatory. One either leaves the old stems on the plants to obtain early flowers, or removes the old spent growth from the previous season, making way for the new growth on which flowers will be borne.

Group One. The species and cultivars that fit into this group produce their flowers on short flower stalks directly from a leaf axil bud, generally on stems produced the previous season which became ripened by the early autumn. The clematis in this group consist of the evergreen species and their cultivated forms, the *alpina* and *macropetala* types and the *montana* group. This group produce their flowers directly from the old stems and, therefore, pruning must not be carried out until all flowering has been completed.

Pruning for this group consists of removing all dead and weak stems immediately after flowering. Established plants five metres high or more are not normally pruned, especially if they are growing in trees. All stems should be tied into position or attached to their host immediately after pruning. If any of the *montana* group have become untidy, or have out-grown their allotted space, then this too is the time for any thinning out or severe pruning that may be required, again remembering to firmly attach remaining stems to the host or support. After pruning, new growth will be produced which will become ripened during the late summer and produce its main crop of flowers the following spring.

Group Two. Clematis in this

GROUP ONE CLEMATIS

1. Flowers appear on short flower stalks directly from a leaf axil bud, generally on stems ripened the previous season.

2. After flowering, new growth is naturally produced which, in turn, will ripen before winter.

3. Flowers will apear from these buds in the following season.

GROUP TWO CLEMATIS

1. Previous season's growth
2. Current season's growth

GROUP THREE CLEMATIS

1. Current season's growth

Flower Development

The nodding flowers of Clematis alpina 'Constance' are replaced with attractive seed heads.

group produce their flowers on the old or previous season's stems and consist of the early, large-flowered cultivars, the double and semi-double and mid-season, large-flowered cultivars. The flowers are borne on single stems which vary from 10cm to 90cm in length. Whether the stems that produce the flowers are short or long, the first flowers are always produced from the previous season's ripened stems.

The observant gardener will notice the swelling leaf axil buds during the late winter onwards. These will have become fat and ready to burst into leaf in early spring and are the buds that grow during the spring months and produce the first crop of flowers from the beginning of early summer. To the experienced gardener the clematis plants will be pointing out where pruning is needed and that is just above where these strong leaf axil buds are visible.

The pruning requirements of this group consist of removing all dead and weak stems, and shortening the remainder by 15–25cm to where a strong pair of leaf axil buds are apparent. All old leaf stalks that still remain

should be removed and all remaining stems should then be tied into position immediately after pruning. The position for tying-in the stems is important and each stem should be given sufficient space where all anticipated new growth and flowers can expand to the full without overcrowding or too much overlapping of growth. When the clematis stems are being tied on to a host plant, be careful not to tie too tightly as this will only cause damage to the clematis and its host in later months, or years if metal ties are used. The pruning and tying-in of stems should be carried out during the late winter or early spring before bud break when weather permits. It is best not to prune during frosty weather both from the point of view of one's fingers and the health of the clematis!

Group Three. The third group contains the section of clematis which produce their flowers on new stems each year and in most cases each stem produces several flowers. The previous season's top growth becomes useless and dies away naturally each winter (unless the winter is a very mild one with little or no frost occurring, when the growth may remain partially alive). Therefore, all previous season's top growth must be removed to allow the current season's stems room to grow to maturity. This clean-cut, tidy up of the plant also removes any stems which may have become infected with mildew, or any other disease during the autumn, thereby giving the plant a fresh start each year.

The time for pruning is again during the later winter or early spring before bud break depending on weather conditions. The actual pruning consists of removing all old top growth down to where the strong new leaf axil buds appear, at a point just above the base of the previous season's stems, approximately within 75cm of soil level. The previous season's stems are identified by their mid-brown colouring, the older stems will be a much paler, light brown-grey colour. Many produce new stems from below the soil level each spring and this should be and is encouraged by hard pruning.

The clematis which are included within this group contain the x *jackmanii* types and late-flowering, large-flowered cultivars, the *viticella* group, the *texensis* group and other late flowering species, including the herbaceous types.

An impatient gardener is sometimes tempted during a very mild winter to prune this type of clematis soon after Christmas. In my experience, it is unwise to be so tempted because the strong, fat leaf axil bud may be encouraged to start growing after pruning only to be severely damaged by a sudden change in the weather. In most cases, if damage does not occur to these buds, the flowers are malformed and useless; so be patient, unless your climate is a mild one. He who hesitates in this case is not lost, but is wise!

Pruning clematis in cold climates

In extremely cold climates the pruning of clematis will be very different for some types of clematis to the advice given above. Where temperatures are expected to drop annually below 10°F (–12°C) the top growth of most of the early large flowered, including the double and semi-double types, (Group Two) can be expected to be damaged to some degree. The amount of damage will depend upon the duration of the winter and whether there is snow cover or how free-draining the soil conditions are. Therefore pruning of the Group Two clematis in these countries will vary from year to year. My advice is to leave all top growth intact until the winter appears to have ended and before bud break. At this time a decision can be made, depending upon the damage caused by the winter weather, about how hard to prune back the remaining top growth. If the winter has been

kind then some ripened leaf axil buds from the previous season will be remaining. If this is the case then the old top growth can be removed down to a strong pair of leaf axil buds which in turn will produce those long awaited early large flowers.

If the winter has been severe then the top growth will need to be cut down to soil level where new growth will appear later in the spring, resulting in late and smaller flowers that year.

The *alpina* types will not be affected by severe winters, the *montanas* may not survive (see more under the chapter on growing clematis in northern climates, page 69), and therefore at best some of the hardier forms may retain some top growth. The early large flowered types (Group Two) will be damaged as described above, the mid season and Group Three clematis can be expected to be reduced down

to soil level, which is normal for those types, so their pruning requirements remain unaltered.

Pruning established clematis

Established clematis which have not received the correct pruning needed for their particular type during cultivation and have become untidy, or bare at the base, are regrettably apparent in large numbers. After reading the pruning recommendations here one must not take a pair of secateurs to a late-flowering (Group Three) type and cut it down to within 75cm of soil level as this would, in most cases, be fatal. Due to incorrect pruning such a plant would most probably not have any active leaf axil buds within 75cm of soil level. My advice for such a plant is to remove all dead and weak stems to where active leaf axil buds appear, at whatever height this may be. As new growth is produced, this may be

Prune above the leaf axil bud.

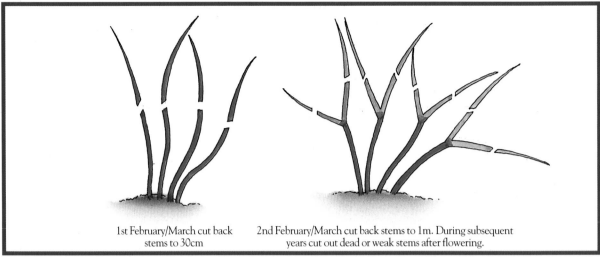

1st February/March cut back
stems to 30cm

2nd February/March cut back stems to 1m. During subsequent
years cut out dead or weak stems after flowering.

Group One

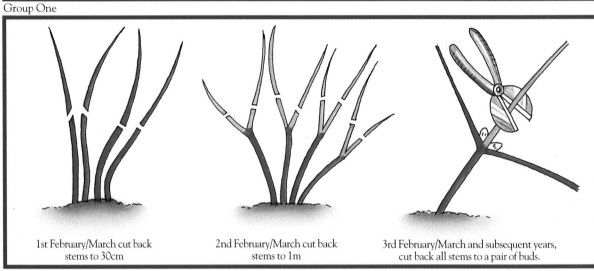

1st February/March cut back
stems to 30cm

2nd February/March cut back
stems to 1m

3rd February/March and subsequent years,
cut back all stems to a pair of buds.

Group Two

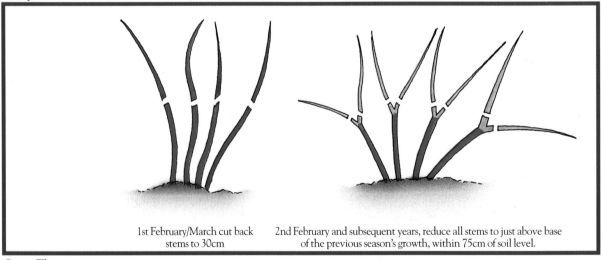

1st February/March cut back
stems to 30cm

2nd February and subsequent years, reduce all stems to just above base
of the previous season's growth, within 75cm of soil level.

Group Three

Pruning Requirements

trained downwards to give annual cover to the bare, lower parts of the clematis. This will most probably be an annual job to attain an attractive plant.

An alternative possible cure, especially with a *montana* type or a large plant of any of the *alpina* or *macropetala* types, is to layer a stem into the soil by carefully disentangling a stem from the mass of growth and slowly bending the stem down to soil level. Layering is detailed on page 73. This will achieve fresh, healthy foliage at the base of the plant and cover up the unsightly bare base of the clematis. It is important that the successfully layered clematis should be pruned back hard in the early spring for the first two years so that a bushy base is achieved. If this practice is not possible, then the simple answer is to purchase another young plant and train it into the base of the older plant.

With an established clematis of the large-flowered cultivar type (Group Two) which has become very bare at its base, there is another alternative cure that can be tried, if the plant has several stems from the base or ground level. As it would be most unwise to cut all stems down to ground level at one time in order to

help regenerate the plant, it is possible to do this in stages. If the plant has several stems or even two growing from soil level, then I suggest that half of the stems are pruned down to approximately 60cm above soil level, just above a node in early spring and just before bud break. It is important that, as these stems are being removed (and some of the top growth may become damaged) care should be taken. If any stems that are to remain are damaged, these should also be cut back to just above an active leaf axil bud. If the hard pruning is successful during the first spring and new growth is achieved, then this exercise can be repeated the following spring. Any new stems that are produced from soil level, or just above, should be pinched back to again achieve a healthy base to the plant.

Another technique which is used by some clematis enthusiasts on clematis from Group Two is to prune these plants back hard (to within 45/60cm of soil level) every third year. In doing this, they regenerate the plant and get rid of any untidy tangle of old top growth. However, the large early flowers have to be given up for one year and the flowering period will be delayed for about four to five weeks.

The clematis will produce smaller flowers, but perhaps more. For the following two seasons, the plants are pruned normally by just removing dead and weak stems and shortening the remaining stems to a strong pair of leaf axil buds.

As mentioned earlier in this chapter my friends in Northern Europe, Northern America and Canada do not have the choice of whether or not to prune their plants of the early large-flowered cultivars (Group Two) as their severe frosts do this for them. So they can only occasionally enjoy the early, very large-flowered clematis, after a very mild winter. Instead of plants such as 'Nelly Moser', 'The President' or 'Lasurstern' flowering during late spring or early summer, they have to wait for their main flush of flowers until later in the summer. Therefore, as one can see, it is possible to experiment with the pruning of clematis as experience is gained and the flowering period can be changed.

The pruning requirements for clematis grown as container plants, for ground cover, or over heathers and other special planting schemes should be checked under those individual headings.

Growing Clematis Through Trees Shrubs and Roses

Clematis suitable for growing over and through trees fortunately amount to quite a cross-section of types. The early and late-flowering species, which rampage to seven metres or more and their respective cultivated forms, allow us a good freedom of choice.

Evergreen trees

Most members of the pine family may be graced with the many strands and flowers of the *montana* forms. The montanas grow eventually up to ten metres or more and look superb when they are in full flower, appearing like a white or pink waterfall as their many vines come cascading down over the branches of the large Corsican pine, or similar sized host.

The growing of clematis underneath trees is rather more difficult than in an open position due to the dry soil conditions. However, if soil preparation as described on page 13 is carried out and adequate water is provided until the clematis becomes established, the gardener will be duly rewarded in the following years. Don't forget that establishment may take two growing seasons and in some very dry positions even three years from planting. When planting under a large tree such as a pine, a site within 30cm of the tree trunk is the most suitable position: see the diagram on page 14.

The newly produced clematis stems can then be tied into position by the use of wires until they reach into the framework of the tree's branches and attach themselves by the use of their leaf stalks (or petioles). The strength of the clematis vines will not be suffi-cient to cause damage to the tree.

Clematis montana and its forms were thought to be extremely winter hardy in the British Isles until the severe frosts of the early 1980s when many plants were killed completely after experiencing temperatures as low

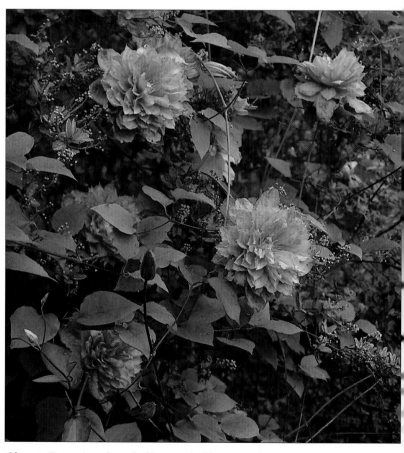

Clematis 'Proteus' can have double, semi-double or single flowers.

'Royal Velvet' is free flowering with velvet purple flowers and dark red anthers.

as −26°C in some parts of England. Work is being carried out to select the most hardy form or cultivar.

Suitable combinations

The most hardy white *montana* is the form currently being sold as *montana f. grandiflora*. This plant grows most successfully in Bavaria, withstanding temperatures as low as −20°C and still flowering freely the following spring. Obviously, it is most unusual for such cold conditions to be normally experienced in England and one should not be put off growing the other forms of montana. But in cold districts, it is useful to know that *montana f. grandiflora* will survive the most extreme winters in the British Isles. This hardy form has flowers with a diameter of 6/8cm and is a good, clear free-flowering white.

Another large-flowered white with more rounded full flowers is C.

montana 'Alexander'; this plant also has good, large leaflets. There are some very poor forms of white *montana* in cultivation which have been grown from seed—always select a good named cultivar. This also applies to the soft pink *montana*. 'Elizabeth' is particularly pleasant with soft pink flowers which are a little gappy but have a lovely scent. Slightly deeper coloured and stronger scented is 'Pink Perfection'. 'Odorata', an old form I found in Sweden, has a delightful vanilla scent and is also pale pink. Two more recently introduced montanas are 'Freda' and 'Mayleen'. *Clematis montana* 'Freda' has extremely dark pinkish-red flowers and most attractive dark bronze foliage. *Clematis montana* 'Mayleen' has pale pink flowers which are produced extremely free and have the strongest scent of any of the *montana* cultivars that I grow. *Clematis montana* 'Tetrarose' has most attractive bronze foliage as well but additional attractions are the large serrated leaves. The flowers of this cultivar are possibly the largest of the pink montana types, being a good 5/7cm in diameter. *Montana* 'Picton's Variety' is possibly the most compact growing of all the pink *montanas*, growing only to about 6 metres.

Clematis chrysocoma (white and pink forms) and *vedrariensis* 'Highdown' are both closely related to the *montanas* but are not so vigorous, growing only to about 6/7 metres. All of the *montana* types flower during late spring and early summer and grow, with the above exceptions, up to 8/10 metres or sometimes more in very favourable conditions. The two latter clematis and *montana* 'Picton's Variety' are suitable for growing through evergreens such as a large *thuya* or lawson's cypress and its many ornamental forms, green, golden or even the various grey-foliaged forms, all of which offer a perfect background to the pink flowers of the clematis.

When the *montana* types are being

grown in large evergreens and the initial hard pruning has been carried out to encourage the plant to become bushy at its base, they can be then left unpruned. If any stems become unattached from the branches of the tree then the ideal time for pruning and tying-in of the stems is immediately after flowering. This will then give the plant time to make new growth so that the following year's crop of flowers is not unduly affected by pruning.

Evergreen hollies can be graced with the tumbling blossoms of the later flowering species and small-flowered cultivars. *Clematis flammula*, a starry, white-flowered scented species from Southern Europe, looks magnificent when in full flower: the stems appear to be clothed with flowers and show up well against the dark green foliage of a holly. Many of the other pale-flowered clematis such as the white 'Huldine', with its freely produced 6cm diameter flowers, also look well growing through an open-branched holly.

The yellow variegated holly trees lend themselves also to show up the flowers of the colourful *viticella* cultivars. Among the attractive range of *viticella* clematis, 'Abundance' wine red, 'Kermesina' deep red, 'Royal Velours' velvet purple, 'Etoile Violette' purple with prominent yellow centre and the similar coloured 'Blue Belle' which has larger flowers, are some of the best for growing in association with the lighter coloured variegated hollies.

Due to the form of a holly tree and the importance of its appearance during the winter months, a late-flowering species or cultivar should be used, so that the larger part of the spent clematis growth can be removed during the later autumn allowing the holly to look tidy during the winter months with the final pruning of the clematis being completed during the early spring before bud break.

Yews, especially the large open

The beauty of this tree is being added to by the careful training of Clematis 'Comtesse de Bouchaud' into it.

trees, not the carefully trimmed ones, also lend themselves to the rampaging species. *C. potanini* var. 'Fargesii', a fine white clematis with 3cm diameter flowers which are produced in abundance from early summer onwards, looks delightful when it has reached a height of six metres on a yew and is in full flower. The delicate, nodding white flowers of *viticella* 'Alba Luxurians' look splendid against the dark background of the old English yew. This clematis is slightly unusual due to each tepal having a green tip, the centre being a deep purple black and the flowers semi-campanulate in form. As one can imagine from the description, it is a little out of the ordinary and well worth a position in a large garden. Due to the important appearance of the yew during the winter months, the lengthy stems of the late-flowering clematis may be reduced in late autumn, with the final and correct pruning being carried out during early spring before bud break. The *montana*

family, I feel, should not be grown over yews, purely because of the untidiness of the old growth during the winter months, and this is why I recommend the later-flowering species and cultivars for appearance and ease of cultivation. As well as the white-flowering species *potanini* var. 'Fargesii',*viticella* 'Alba Luxurians' both previously mentioned, 'Huldine' and *flammula* are also white and lend themselves to be grown and flower against the dark foliage of a large yew. Our native clematis commonly known as "old man's beard" or "traveller's joy", *Clematis vitalba*, also needs a dark background to display its many thousands of creamy white flowers. The masses of silky seed heads from which the common names have obviously derived look best when the stems, which grow to nine metres, can be allowed to clamber up a tree.

Clematis serratifolia, which is similar to the more commonly grown *C. tibetana* and it forms, also looks well on a dark background. This vigorous species from Korea grows to six metres in height and has pale yellow flowers which are nodding and composed of four tepals with a central tuft of deep purple-red anthers. The flowers are produced from late summer until the first autumn frosts. The hawthorn scented blossoms of C. *terniflora* formerly C. *maximowicziana*, again white, need the framework of a large tree to display its flowers. The species which attains six metres of growth needs a hot sunny position to flower well in the British Isles. Until several years ago it had been known as C. *paniculata* and in more recent years C. *maximowicziana* however it has been corrected once more to *terniflora*. In the United States of America the plant is still incorrectly called *paniculata*.

For the garden which contains only a moderate sized conifer, yew or similar type of evergreen tree, some of the mid-season large-flowered cultivars and the later-flowering cultivars may be successfully used to add colour and a variation to the white-flowered species that need at least a ten metre high tree. Of the mid-season flowering clematis, the pale blues such as 'W. E. Gladstone', 'Mrs Bush' and 'Mrs Hope', the pale pink 'Fairy Queen' or the pale mauve of 'King Edward VII' and the large-flowered whites 'Marie Boisselot' and 'Henryi' may be utilised. The pruning requirements of these large-flowered cultivars, if grown in such a situation, need to be changed and they can be pruned fairly hard in the early spring before bud break to encourage plenty of new growth. Some old stems to the height of one-and-a-half to two metres should be left to produce the early flowers. The hard pruned stems will then produce flowers later, during the summer months. The late, large-flowered cultivars such as 'Comtesse de Bouchaud' and 'Hagley Hybrid', both of which are pink-mauve, and the

semi-campanulate, pale blue flowers of 'Perle d'Azur', may also be used to add colour and interest to the dark background of a yew which will display their pale coloured flowers to best advantage.

Pruning clematis on evergreen trees

The gardener unaccustomed to growing clematis through other plants, shrubs and trees may be slightly worried and concerned about damage to the host when pruning is to be carried out. As mentioned earlier, clematis stems attach themselves by the leaf stalk (petiole) but this attachment is slowly reduced when the winter months approach. After several frosts the foliage of the deciduous clematis starts to decay and falls from the plant, leaving the leaf stalk loosely attached to the host. By early winter, when I recommend that the Group Three types have their top growth reduced to leave the yew, conifers or other evergreen in a tidy state for the remaining winter months, the leaf stalks will come away from their support without causing damage. There is no need to use a pair of garden steps to reach the top growth of the clematis which may have reached a height of five metres or so. The severed stems may be gently, but firmly, tugged from the tree or shrub, causing virtually no damage, and then burnt. The final and correct pruning may then be carried out during early spring before bud break as weather conditions permit. This double type of pruning when the top growth is reduced to one-and-a-half metres or so in early winter is, in fact, an advantage. It ensures that a good selection of active leaf axil buds is available when final pruning is carried out in early spring, and will keep the plant bushy and well furnished at its base.

Deciduous trees

Whereas the soft and hardwood evergreens lend themselves beautifully to

hosting clematis, regrettably the deciduous hardwoods, such as oak, elm, sycamore, planes, limes, etc., do not, due to the nature of their structure. Also, in my opinion, the appearance of these elegant and graceful trees would be spoilt with climbers of any type clambering about their branches.

However, deciduous trees the size and shape of the flowering cherry, *Sorbus*, lilac, *Laburnum*, *Robinia*, even old cherry, damson, pear or apple trees that have passed their best regarding fruiting, but are retained in the garden because of their character and shapes, are ideal. Any one of these types of tree may be successfully used to host the stems of a clematis giving the necessary support and allowing the flowers to be shown to their best advantage. The erect-growing *Prunus* 'Amanogawa' which grows in a slender column needs the addition of another plant to give it colour during the period when its flowers have passed their best. The pale pink flowers of 'Comtesse de Bouchaud' look refreshing as they trail from this *Prunus* at two metres high and further upwards as the season progresses. The late-flowering species and late-flowering, large-flowered cultivars are the most successful for smallish, deciduous trees. The reason for this is again because I like a garden, however natural it may be, to appear under control during the winter months. Therefore the late-flowering clematis may be provisionally tied up during early winter with final pruning being carried out at the correct time in early spring as described under the Evergreen Tree section.

Selecting and positioning your clematis

The selection of species or cultivar must depend upon individual taste but choice of flower colour, foliage association and the actual tree being used should all be taken into account.

However, there are several additional points that need to be considered. The first is that the host tree should be studied regarding the position of the clematis planting site because the clematis branches will naturally grow towards the sun on the lightest side of a small tree where they will then flower. Therefore, on a small tree some training of stems during the early part of each summer is required, so that one can then select the flowering position, because if left to nature the vines will grow into the lightest area which may not be the most effective place.

On a large tree, where the the total circumference is much greater, the position where the clematis will flower can be more easily pre-determined due to the fact that the stems will mostly grow and flower on the side they are planted. When considering the flowering position of a clematis it is important, therefore, to consider both the height and type of a host tree and the height of the clematis. As a guide, the ultimate height of the late, large-flowered cultivars varies between two-and-a-half and four metres, and the species vary from about three metres in height.

The density and colour of foliage of the tree is another important factor. For instance, if the foliage is pale coloured as with *Pyrus salicifolia* 'Pendula' (the silver-foliaged weeping pear), a purple clematis such as the free-flowering *viticella* 'Etoile Violette' or the ever popular 'Jackmanii Superba' may be used, but if the foliage is very dark, as with a pear or thickly branched apple tree, one must choose a pale-flowered clematis such as 'Comtesse de Bouchaud', 'Huldine' or the pale-flowered *viticella* cultivars 'Minuet', 'Margot Koster', 'Little Nell' or 'Alba Luxurians'.

As a further guideline, the following planting association, using a medium sized deciduous tree and one of the late-flowering large or small-flowered cultivars, may be considered. The au-

This ceanothus is a good companion for Clematis 'Maureen'.

tumn-flowering cherry *Prunus subhirtella* 'Autumnalis Rosea' is an ideal, open-branched, lightly foliaged tree giving the correct support and framework, where one of the *viticella* cultivars such as 'Abundance', 'Madame Julia Correvon', 'Kermesina' or 'Soderaltje' (formerly 'Grandiflora Sanguinea') can be shown to great advantage. In this instance one is adding colour to the tree during mid to late summer, but the main clematis top growth is removed before the cherry commences flowering.

The golden foliage of *Robinia pseudoacacia* 'Frisia' is an absolute must to display the purple flowers of either *viticella* 'Etoile Violette' which produces masses of medium sized flowers, the new larger-flowered *viticella* 'Polish Spirit' with purple-blue flowers or, alternatively, 'Gipsy Queen' with large, deep purple flowers; these clematis flower from mid summer onwards. To enhance the dense foliage of a *Laburnum*, one should choose a free-flowering clematis such as the *viticella* cultivars: 'Margot Koster' with pale

rosy-red flowers, or 'Minuet' with delightful white flowers veined throughout with mauve. The contrast of the purple flowers of 'Jackmanii Superba' or the carmine-red flowers of 'Ville de Lyon', will also give much-needed colour to a *Laburnum* tree from mid summer until early autumn. *Sorbus cashmiriana*, with its fern-like foliage, is an ideal host for late-flowering cultivars like 'Star of India', a very free-flowering deep purple-blue, and the rosy purple flowers of 'Victoria'. The clematis add colour and interest to the *Sorbus* after its flowering time and before the glistening white berries in the autumn.

Large shrubs
Both evergreen and deciduous shrubs lend themselves to hosting clematis The list of suitable hosts in this section could be nearly endless. I must, therefore, leave the final decisions of combination to the imaginative gardener; but again there are some guidelines that may assist with the choice of host and the selection of the correct

type of clematis.

The large-flowered cultivar and tall-growing species rhododendrons lend themselves perfectly to the support of the twining stems of a clematis. The mid-season, large-flowered cultivars need such a host so that their natural, free growing, open framework of stems can spread themselves, distributing their very large open flowers widely over their support. This group of clematis produces flowers on the previous season's and current season's stems and this must be remembered when the clematis is being trained during the growing season. Some of the best mid-season, large-flowered cultivars which grow successfully with rhododendrons are the lavender-blue of 'Masquerade' or the slightly paler blue 'Belle Nantaise'. The superb 'Marie Boisselot' with large white blooms or the pale lavender of 'Peveril Pearl' all lend themselves well to this plant association as does 'Violet Charm' with its pale blue flowers with red anthers when grown with the pink flowers species, *syringa*.

Medium sized shrubs

A selection of early, large-flowered cultivars, double, and semi-double cultivars may also be used to grow through rhododendrons or a similar type of shrub which is not more than five metres high. The proposed host should not have an open framework of branches where wind can blow directly through the host, causing distress to the clematis vines by detaching them from their support. Due to the flowering of this selection of clematis and the closeness of each flower to one another and the shortness of the stems, the host needs to be compact. *Rhododendron*, cotoneaster, (the large-leafed densely branched types) large *pyracanthas*, *escallonias*, and other free standing deciduous shrubs including established Japanese maples, *Cercidiphyllum*, *Cercis*, *Cotinus* and *Cytisus battandieri* are all suitable hosts.

Of the early large-flowered clematis, a selection of the following cultivars will give a good range of colours: 'Barbara Jackman', blue with petunia bars, 'Elsa Späth' mid-blue, 'John Warren' deep pink, 'Kathleen Wheeler' deep plummy-mauve, 'Lasurstern' clear blue, 'Lincoln Star' pink striped, 'Lord Nevill' deep blue, 'Nelly Moser' mauve-pink, 'Niobe' red, 'The President' purple-blue and 'William Kennett' pale blue. Of the slightly newer cultivars, 'Gillian Blades', which is white with a hint of pale blue, has beautiful wavy edges to the tepals which are pale blue, making a very full

flower, also with creamy white anthers, and is particularly long flowering; 'Fireworks' lives up to its name with a full display of colourful flowers of purple and red with red anthers.

Cultivars of more recent introduction from our nursery which should be mentioned here are 'Anna Louise' named after my second daughter which has striking and dramatically coloured violet flowers with a contrasting red/purple bar and red anthers, 'Royal Velvet' which has a very free flowering habit throughout the summer months with rich velvet purple flowers and red anthers, 'Sugar

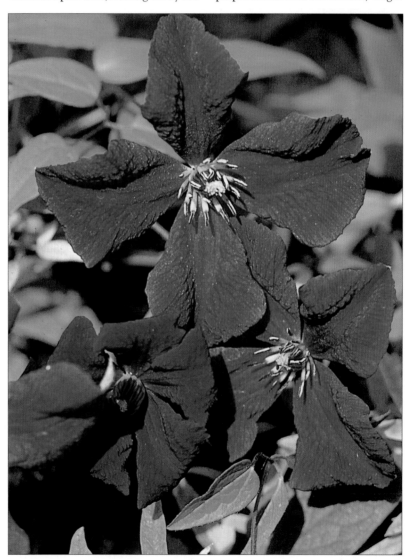

Clematis viticella 'Polish Spirit' is a new and very free-flowering cultivar.

Grey foliaged companion plants and deep red clematis flowers always look striking together: Clematis viticella 'Royal Velours'.

Candy' with large pale pink flowers with a darker central stripe and yellow anthers and the 1995 introduction 'Liberation' with deep reddish pink flowers also with a darker central band and yellow anthers.

Double and semi-double cultivars which may be used include 'Beauty of Worcester' deep blue, 'Proteus' mauve, 'Vyvyan Pennell' purple-mauve and the semi-doubles 'Lady Caroline Nevill' pale lavender and 'Mrs George Jackman' white. Another semi-double white is 'Sylvia Denny', with tightly formed rosette-like flowers on the old wood in spring

and single flowers on current season's wood, later in the summer. An old cultivar that should not be missed out is 'Belle of Woking' with slightly mauve-white, fully double flowers and, of course, the newer semi-double 'Royalty' with rich purple-mauve flowers and yellow anthers in the spring and single flowers during the later summer months.

Possibly the best of all the double clematis is our 1994 introduction 'Arctic Queen' which produces most freely double white flowers both from old or new growth. The amount of flower this new cultivar produces is

staggering from early summer until the end of the autumn months.

Mid-season cultivars include 'King Edward VII' puce-violet, 'Marie Boisselot' white, 'Maureen' purple and 'Serenata' rich purple. If desired a selection of late-flowering cultivars can also be used to give a longer and more varied flowering period through the season: cultivars such as 'Ascotiensis' blue, 'Ernest Markham' red, 'Gipsy Queen' rich purple, 'Jackmanii Superba' purple-blue, 'Madame Edouard André' dusky red, 'Perle d'Azur' pale blue and 'Ville de Lyon' carmine red. The *viticella* cultivars may also be added to the list of possible varieties to choose from, giving a good variation of habit and flowering periods for the gardener with a large garden who is in need of a continuity of flowers from May until the end of September.

Plant associations that I have found most satisfying include the use of *Pyracantha rogersiana* 'Flava', whose bright green leaves are a pleasant background to the plummy-purple flowers of 'Kathleen Wheeler'. The purple foliage of *Acer palmatum* 'Atropurpureum' is a superb foil to the pink flowers of 'John Warren', or the pale lavender flowers of 'Mrs Cholmondeley'. *Cotinus* 'Foliis Purpureis' or *Cotinus* 'Royal Purple', with their outstanding purple foliage, display the flowers of 'Nelly Moser' mauve-pink, 'Perle d'Azur' pale blue and the white flowers of 'Mrs George Jackman' to great advantage. The choice of *Cytisus battandieri* and 'Victoria' is a delightful combination when the silver-grey leaves of the *Cytisus* are looking their best and the yellow pineapple-like flowers of the shrub and the rosy purple flowers of the clematis are all performing at the same time. The association of *Clematis* 'Marie Boisselot' and the grey-green foliage of *Cotoneaster franchetti* is also very desirable. And, of course, a delightful combination can be achieved by growing the free-flowering *Clematis* 'Niobe' through the various forms of variegated dogwood (*Cornus*): the combination of its rich red flowers and the delicate variegated foliage and red stems of the host is a must.

Shorter growing shrubs

Compact, more densely branched shrubs such as some varieties of *Pyracantha*, compact forms of *Cotoneaster*, evergreen *Ceanothus*, *Camellia*, *Aucuba*, which may be free standing or wall trained, are all satisfactory hosts for the early large-flowered cultivars and the double cultivars which, due to the size and density of their flowers, require protection from the wind. The selection of clematis in this case needs thought: one must take into consideration the flowering time of the host; one must decide if the clematis should flower before, with, or after the host has flowered; and the colour of the flower and foliage of both host and clematis are vitally important considerations.

A selection of clematis for compact, lower-growing evergreen shrubs includes the early, large-flowered cultivars such as 'Asao' pale pink, 'Pink Champagne' (Kakio) deep mauve-pink, 'Barbara Dibley' petunia red, 'Bees Jubilee' pink mauve striped, 'Corona' purplish pink, 'Dawn' pearly white, 'Edith' white with a prominent red centre, 'H F Young' Wedgwood blue, 'Horn of Plenty' mauve, 'Lady Londesborough' pale blue, 'Lady Northcliffe' clear blue, 'Miss Bateman' white, 'Mrs N Thompson' blue with red stripes, 'Mrs P B Truax' periwinkle blue. The new cultivars which have a compact free flowering habit are 'Guernsey Cream' creamy yellow, 'Anna Louise' violet with contrasting red/purple bar, 'Royal Velvet' rich velvet purple and 'Masquerade' lavender rosy-blue. Two older cultivars now becoming more widely available are 'Snow Queen' white with rosy to blue tints and 'Ruby Glow' with glowing ruby red tepals.

The deep red flowers of Clematis viticella 'Kermesina' contrast well with this conifer.

Double and semi-doubles which flower from early summer onwards include 'Countess of Lovelace' pale blue, 'Duchess of Edinburgh' white, 'Vyvyan Pennell' purple-mauve and the semi-double 'Daniel Deronda' purple-blue and the outstanding new 'Arctic Queen' with clear white flowers.

A selection of some of the later-flowering cultivars which flower from mid summer onwards may also be used to give an added colour range and continuity of flowering. Some of the most satisfactory are: 'Ascotiensis' bright blue, 'Comtesse de Bouchaud' pink-mauve, 'Gipsy Queen' deep purple, 'Hagley Hybrid' rosy pink, 'Madame Edouard André' dusky red, 'Perle d'Azur' pale blue, 'Victoria' rosy purple and 'Ville de Lyon' carmine red, and the striking new cultivars 'Liberation' deep pinkish red and 'Sugar Candy' pink-striped. *Texensis* cultivars 'Duchess of Albany' cherry-pink, 'Gravetye Beauty' ruby-red and the fascinating new 'Petit Faucon'

with its semi-campanulate small deep blue flowers also extend the selection of shapes, sizes and colour range from which the discerning gardener can choose.

The low-growing shrubs which do not attain a greater height than two metres force the clematis to display their flowers below this height. Thus one does not have to look upwards to the sky to view the flowers at close quarters as with some of the previous plant association recommendations.

Cotoneaster microphyllus, grown as a free standing shrub, rarely attains more that just over a metre in height, making an ideal host plant on which the *texensis* cultivars 'Duchess of Albany' and 'Gravetye Beauty' and 'Sir Trevor Lawrence' can display the miniature tulip-like flowers which need to be looked directly into to gain the full pleasure of their unusual shape. The slightly grey foliage of *Cotoneaster buxifolius vellaeus* is a splendid foil to enhance the pale pearly-white flowers of 'Dawn' which are produced

The old favourite 'Nelly Moser' has a lush backdrop of green, wall trained shrubs.

the new cultivar 'Royal Velvet' which will give the same effect but earlier in the summer.

Clematis in association with roses

The use of clematis with wall-trained, pillar or climbing roses on pergolas or archways can be most effective, each offering its companion either support or colour when the other is not in flower, thus gaining maximum effect from a small area of one's garden. The association can also be carried through to the garden where roses are grown as free-standing shrubs.

Every year the use of roses as shrubs is increasing. The old-fashioned shrub roses include the splendid Gallicas, Albas, Damasks, Centifolia and Moss roses, all of which are easily placed in a modern garden either in groups, hedges or as specimen plants. The hybrid teas, and to a slightly lesser extent the cluster roses, are more difficult to place in a garden if one wants to get away from the typical way of planting roses like soldiers in rows. The delightful "old roses" give us colour, form and scent, but regrettably have a limited flowering period as compared with the cluster roses, although their framework of branches and foliage gives us the ideal support for the large-flowered clematis. Due to the pruning requirement of the roses the late large-flowering cultivars are the best, thus avoiding the conflict of clematis stems to remain and rose stem to be removed. The gardener who knows his old roses may well use some of the early large-flowered cultivars through some of the roses which require less pruning. Once again, if the experienced gardener requires to use a particular clematis cultivar because of the colour of the flowers, then the early-flowering cultivar may be pruned harder than generally recommended with the result that the flowering period will be delayed, the large early flowers being lost, but the desired

from early summer onwards. Both cotoneasters have a low arching habit and dainty leaves which cluster around the stems, giving an interesting contrast in foliage shape and colour, as well as emphasising the obvious attraction of the clematis flowers. Plants of *Ceanothus* 'Autumnal Blue' are occasionally grown as a free-standing shrub in mild localities, and the glossy green evergreen leaves plus the powder-blue flowers which appear from early summer onwards offer the possibility of hosting several clematis, all of which can either flower before the ceanothus or with it. 'Mrs N Thompson', 'Vyvyan Pennell', 'Liberation' or 'Sugar Candy' all early summer flowering, will also produce their second crop of flowers while the ceanothus is flowering. The semi-double 'Daniel Deronda' will produce its deep purple-blue flowers before and while the host is flowering. The mauve-pink

flowers of 'Comtesse de Bouchaud' are produced while the ceanothus is in flower, giving an even greater combination of colours.

The grey foliage of *Brachyglottis greyi* presents itself beautifully to show off the contrasting colour of early-flowering cultivars such as 'H F Young' Wedgwood blue, the white flowers of 'Artic Queen', the rosy mauve of 'Hagley Hybrid' or even the dusky red flower of 'Madame Edouard André'.

Another marvellous combination using a grey foliage shrub and a clematis is a planting association between *Phlomis fruticosa*, with its thick grey leaves and pale yellow flowers, and the old clematis cultivar 'Madame Grangé', with its deep plummy-purple flowers. This super old plant usually has six tepals that are somewhat boat shaped, never opening fully, which gives it additional charm and interest. A similar colour combination is to use result of colour association will be achieved. The *x jackmanii* types such as 'Ascotiensis', 'Comtesse de Bouchaud', 'Gipsy Queen', 'Hagley Hybrid', 'Jackmanii Superba', 'Madame Baron Veillard', 'Madame Edouard André', 'Perle d'Azur', 'Star of India' and 'Victoria' offer various shades from blue, pink, red and purple, all of which blend well with the flowers of the shrub roses.

Another good successful association that I've seen was achieved by underplanting a bed of pink and red cluster roses with *Clematis x jackmanii* and *Clematis integrifolia*. The large purple flowers of *x jackmanii* look fascinating popping up through the roses. The nodding mid-blue flowers of the herbaceous *C. integrifolia* also look fun scrambling around just beneath the roses or just clambering up into the lower stems. The pink *integrifolia* 'Rosea' or the rarer but beautifully scented white *integrifolia Alba* would also blend well with the correct shades of the cluster roses.

And so the combinations and planting can go on, creating a picture in one's mind one year, planting the next and hopefully seeing the realisation the following year and for many years to come. With a little imagination and careful selections of both host and clematis and good cultivation, one can achieve most satisfactory results.

These plants grouped together make a striking combination. They are Clematis 'Gipsy Queen' and 'Bees Jubilee' with Abutilon striatum.

Using Clematis as Ground Cover

Only a few clematis are capable of complete ground cover, in the sense of the true meaning of the word, which is "to cover and smother the ground". When clematis species are found growing in the wild they either scramble around at ground level and eventually locate a suitable support on to which they grow and then climb to possibly flop back down the support, or climb even higher. From this description one can assume that many of the clematis species are suitable for ground cover, if this term is used loosely.

The smothering types which will sprawl around until a suitable support comes within reach are as follows: *Clematis cirrhosa balearica* and the newly introduced *cirrhosa* 'Freckles' with its larger, deeper spotted flowers. Both of which are evergreen clematis and native of the Mediterranean regions, but regrettably are not completely winter hardy. If they are to be used as successful ground cover, they need an almost frost-free position. They both produce creamy white nodding flowers which have purple blotches in the inside of each tepal.

All of the *alpina* and *macropetala* group naturally scramble and smother at ground level. *Alpina*, a charming European species, has given rise to many cultivars, all of which have single, four tepalled nodding flowers. Some of the most free flowering are 'Columbine' (pale blue), 'Pamela Jackman' (deep blue), 'Frankie' (mid-blue with blue markings on the inner petaloid stamens), 'Helsingborg' (deep purple-blue), 'Ruby' (reddish pink), 'Willy' (pink) and 'Frances Rivis'. This is the largest flowered *alpina* with long, slightly twisted pale blue tepals.

Two of the recently introduced *alpinas*, 'Constance' and 'Pink Flamingo' have almost double flowers. These two with ruby red and pink flowers are a most welcomed addition to this use-

The cultivar 'Dawn' creeps at ground level.

ful group. 'Pink Flamingo' is perhaps the most exciting with pale pink flowers with darker red vein to the base of the tepal, it also has a good long flowering period. Another *alpina* of recent introduction is 'Blue Dancer' with similar coloured flowers to 'Frances Rivis', its tepals are narrower and longer.

Macropetala, which is a native of China, with lavender blue semi-double flowers, has also more recently given rise to a range of cultivars such as 'Blue Bird' (mauve-blue), 'Rosy O'Grady' (pink-mauve), 'Lagoon' (deep violet blue), 'Jan Lindmark' (purple) and 'White Swan' (white). The older 'White Moth' (white) and 'Markham's Pink', an old cultivar, are some of the best of this superb range which look delightful scrambling around at ground level, especially if there is a rock or some form of support to give the plant added height and another dimension. The *alpina* and *macropetala* types will give a cover of approximately three square metres.

Clematis montana and all of its family make a very dense ground cover giving a cover of approximately eight square metres after three years. The reader will recall that this rampaging species can vary from white to various shades of pink, and can climb up to ten metres in a tree, therefore, give your *montana* plant sufficient space to develop and keep it trained after each season's flowers have faded.

Of the late-flowering species which can give very good ground cover, *serratifolia* pale yellow, *tibetana* and *tangutica*, both yellow, are all capable of growing each year to give a ground cover of approximately six square metres. *Clematis glauca akebioides*, a plant similar to *tangutica* in habit but with the added attraction of having glaucous, finely cut foliage, is a little more out of the ordinary. Its flowers are smaller than those of *tangutica* but are produced in masses and are creamy on the inside on the

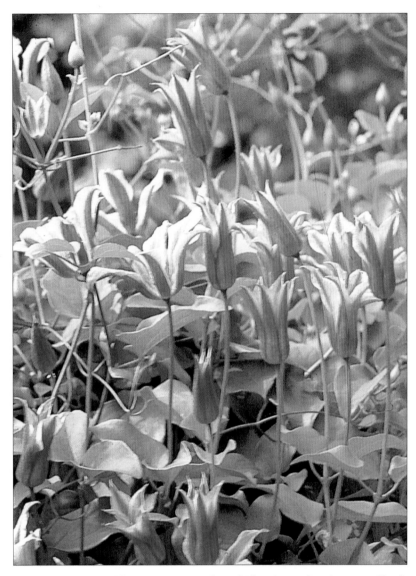

Clematis texensis 'Duchess of Albany' grows happily at ground level.

tepal and slightly bronzy on the outside, giving the plant an interesting colour mix, especially when in full flower. The medium-sized white flowers of 'Huldine' look refreshing against its deep coloured foliage when allowed to scramble at ground level, and is capable of covering five to six square metres annually.

The small-flowered cultivar *Clematis x jouiniana* and its early-flowering form 'Praecox' are among the best smothering clematis because their foliage is coarse and their leaves are large, which means they give total

ground cover. This cultivar between *Clematis vitalba* ("old man's beard") and *Clematis heracleifolia davidiana* produces delightful, soft lavender hyacinth-like flowers from mid summer onwards. Its range is only about three square metres but it is ideal for ground cover and to scramble over short tree stumps that are in need of camouflage.

As one would imagine, *Clematis vitalba* makes a superb ground cover plant. This species, like all the others in this section, is shown to advantage if allowed to scramble over some form of vertical support. If no natural sup-

Clematis texensis 'Etoile Rose' has a vigorous nature and here has been left to happily scramble over this wall.

port in the form of a rock or natural bank, or rise or fall in the ground level is available, then something should be added. Stout branches of a hardwood tree may be placed in the site, with one end placed into the soil to a depth of 50cm or so to give stability. The branch may be cut to a desired size or shape, and then placed into the soil at an angle to give yet further interest.

From reading several old books on gardening I find that clematis, and in most cases the large-flowered cultivars, were grown on such supports as I've just described. The mind boggles at the thought of seeing clematis grown in this way, as permanent bedding plants in specially selected beds with the added interest of shaped tree branches to give the necessary height. The later, large-flowered cultivars would be best, I feel, because the beds could then be tidied up each spring, when all the previous season's growth could be removed. Mid-season large-flowered cultivars could also be used in this type of scheme and the plants would not come to much harm if they received hard pruning similar to the late flowerers. Their presence would add variety in flower shape, flowering time and colour range.

Personally I feel that a flower border given over entirely to clematis would be rather uninteresting during the winter months, and here the use of several different types of evergreen shrubs would be invaluable. The ones I have in mind are *Cistus x corbariensis* and *x cyprius* 'Silver Pink', *Corokia cotoneaster*, *cotoneaster* varieties like *adpressus* and *buxifolius vellaeus*, any of the broom family as they can look splendid with clematis vines trailing through them especially if there is a breeze, *Cytisus albus* 'Burkwoodii', *nigricans*, *x praecox* and *purpureus*.

Other plants to consider are the evergreen *Daphne retusa*, *Erica mediterranea* 'Superba' a tree heather and *eucalyptus* which are pollarded back each spring and kept as bushes. *Eucalyptus gunnii* makes a splendid winter foliage plant. Also try *Genista lydia* and the

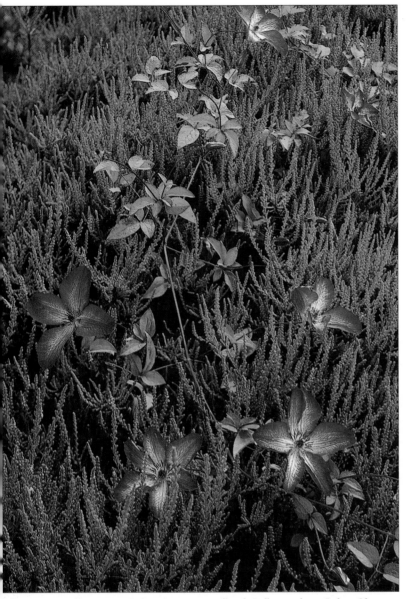

Clematis viticella *Venosa Violacea* contrasts well with Calluna vulgaris *Robert Chaman*.

ter bearing glowing red flowers. The flowers of 'Gravetye Beauty' open slightly more than those of 'Duchess of Albany'. *Clematis x durandii*, a large-flowered non-clinging cultivar with deep indigo-blue flowers with a cream coloured centre, needs the support of a low-growing shrub where its stems can just flop and ramble about. The elegant double flowers of *viticella* 'Purpurea Plena Elegans' show up very well when grown over the rounded form of *Hebe rakaiensis* (*subalpina*) which has fresh, apple-green foliage. A semi-herbaceous *Clematis x aromatica* looks most interesting when it is allowed to scramble over a grey foliage shrub, dispersing its small starry purple flowers over its host. As you can see, the options available to the gardener with imagination and time to plant such planting schemes is vast, if not inexhaustible.

Clematis and heathers

One of the most successful plant associations that I have become aware of is the use of the viticella cultivars to grow over winter-flowering heathers. A large bed of winter-flowering heathers is splendid from late winter onwards; but the flowers of the heathers then fade away, leaving a rather uninteresting carpet of fresh green until the next flowering season. With the use of *viticella* cultivars, the green carpet can be transformed into a very pretty patchwork of colours from mid summer until the early autumn months.

Clematis viticella itself varies in the wild from differing shades of bluish-mauve to white. It was introduced in the 16th century from Central Europe to British gardens and has since given rise to many splendid small-flowered cultivars. The ones most worthy of garden value and for the purpose of planting over heather are as follows: 'Abundance', deep pinky-red, 'Alba Luxurians', a fascinating white form with tepals that reflex, most tepals

evergreen hardy hebes, especially the grey foliaged ones. At the front of such a proposed border the rock roses (*Helianthemum*) can be grown, making a marvellous carpet for odd clematis vines to trail on. *Senecios*, lavenders and the evergreen *Prunus laurocerasus* 'Otto Luyken' could also be used. I feel this gives a sufficient range to choose from which would provide a variety of foliage form, shape of bush and colour of leaf and flower.

Some of the shrubs which I have

recommended for the special clematis border planting idea can also be used as individual hosts for some less rampaging late-flowered species and their cultivars. The American cultivars *viorna*, *pitcheri*, and *texensis* have fascinating urn or pitcher-shaped flowers. The gorgeous *texensis* cultivars 'Duchess of Albany' and 'Gravetye Beauty' have delightful little flowers that give the impression of being miniature tulip flowers—the former having a soft pink flower and the lat-

This old cultivar, Clematis 'Jackmanii Rubra' looks striking growing amongst any grey foliaged plant.

having a green tip, 'Etoile Violette' which has 7cm diameter deep violet flowers with contrasting creamy anthers, 'Little Nell' with creamy white flowers with overtones of mauve, 'Madame Julia Correvon', with wine-red flowers—a rather gappy flower, each tepal twisting and recurving at the tip—'Margot Koster', another gappy-type flower, with deep mauve-pink flowers, 'Minuet' which produces an abundance of semi-nodding flowers that have a white background and mauve veins at the margins, 'Royal Velours' whose flowers are so deep in colour they need the light background of one of the golden foliage heathers to show the flowers to best effect—the flower is a full round shape and the tepals are a deep velvety purple—'Kermesina' with masses of deep wine-red flowers, and lastly the

delightful veined flowers of 'Venosa Violacea' which are the largest of this group, reaching about 7–8cm, in diameter with the boat-shaped tepals veined throughout with purple on a white background that give the flower a very fascinating appearance. *Clematis* 'Sodertalje' (formerly 'Grandiflora Sanguinea') is a useful addition to the range with deep reddish pink-mauve flowers which are 5/6cm in diameter and are semi-campanulate. The new deep purple-blue 'Polish Spirit' is a stunning plant being raised in Poland by Brother Stefan Franczak. This plant is perhaps a little too vigorous for small young heather beds but is ideal for growing up into conifers or large shrubs on the fringe of heathers, allowing a few strands of its delightful flowers to flop over the heathers.

The method for planting the *viti-*

cellas amongst heathers is quite straightforward. The clematis need to be planted at approximately one and a half metres apart and it may be necessary for a heather plant to be removed on an established bed. Soil preparation as described on page 13 should be carried out unless the heather bed was well prepared before planting. If a heather bed, which has only been planted for a few months, is to be used, it is advisable to allow the heathers twelve to eighteen months to become established so that the clematis will not swamp the young heathers.

The clematis, when grown over heathers in this manner, should be pruned back hard in early winter to allow the heathers to start their flowering at the correct time and also to prevent rain-soaked clematis leaves sagging on to the heathers causing

Using Clematis as Ground Cover

harm to their foliage and possibly spoiling their flowers. The amount of clematis growth during the summer months is not sufficient to cause harm and the heathers will not become spoilt or smothered. Due to the earlier than normal pruning of the clematis, new growth may appear early the following year if the winter is at all a mild one. If this is the case, and there are also mice present in the heather border, damage may occur, and the prevention method suggested under the Pest and Diseases section on page 76 should be carried out.

The *viticella* cultivars are equally successful when used to enhance the flowers of the summer-flowering heathers; and in addition to the *viticellas*, the *texensis* cultivars and *x durandii* may also be used to give many interesting flower and colour combinations.

The fascinating 'Petit Faucon' with its semi-campanulate deep royal blue flowers with yellow anthers with its non-clinging habit to about one metre also looks very very dramatic when grown through heathers.

Clematis and annuals

Late, large-flowered cultivars can also be used to scramble through and over many of the summer-flowering, annual bedding plants. *Clematis* 'Jackmanii Superba' looks splendid planted with deep purple-red asters, and the effect is even better if several other taller-growing plants such as woolly-leafed *Helichrysum petiolatum* or the grey-foliaged *senecios* are dot-planted amongst the asters. The range of bedding plants is vast; and I suggest that anyone wishing to try out this particular idea should spend a little time during one summer planning such a border with annuals and the permanent planting of clematis, and looking in other gardens for ideas of plant and colour associations.

Clematis viticella 'Venosa Violacea' brings colour to this juniper.

Clematis in Containers and in the Conservatory

Unfortunately not all gardeners are able to cultivate and grow clematis in the natural manner, with the root system established into good garden soil and the plant able to grow through a suitable host plant. The exciting fact is that some clematis can be grown successfully in a container. Frustrated gardeners who are limited in garden space, people with only small patio gardens, or even those who have to put up with the ever-increasing spread of concrete, can take advantage of growing clematis in this way.

Clematis grown in containers have many uses. They can be used to brighten up dull parts of a concrete yard area, along the walls of buildings that are surrounded by hard stone, or by concrete pathways where no natural soil or flower beds can be prepared for planting. The conservatory, cold glass-house, or even a naturally well-lit living room or garden room lend themselves to the cultivation of certain varieties of clematis for pot or container culture. A 30cm diameter container with an early large-flowered clematis in full flower, with perhaps twenty or thirty blooms, will make an everlasting impression on any gardener's mind, and tempt even the anti-

In order to provide variety in your container use a selection of cultivars when planting.

clematis person into attempting to repeat such a spectacle.

The correct choice of clematis is the most important factor but the correct size and type of container and the right mixture of compost are also vital. Other details such as watering, feeding, training and the general health of the container-grown clematis need careful attention. Such detail and patience is rewarded each spring when the clematis starts into new growth, followed by those handsome, large, colourful flowers.

Choosing your clematis

The choice of clematis species or cultivar is, I feel, the most important decision to be made. This problem is made easier by the fact that the only choice is between those varieties within the early-flowering group. If a container-grown clematis is required for a small patio, sun lounge, garden room or balcony area, the plant should be of a naturally compact, bushy habit and produce its flowers on the old wood, or the previous season's ripened stems. The *alpina* and *macropetala* cultivars, the evergreen types, with the exception of *armandii*, are delightful "pot clematis", but the period of flower is limited. If area and space are not a problem and several different plants are to be grown to flower over an extended period, then the small-flowered types should be tried.

If space is limited and only one or two plants can be grown, then one should rely on the early large flowered cultivars. Within this range there is great choice: in colour, formation of flower and to some extent flowering period. Some of the first ones to flower in this group are 'Anna Louise', 'Asao', 'Dawn', 'Edith' 'Masquerade', 'Miss Bateman', 'Mrs P.B. Traux', 'Pink Champagne' (Kakio), 'Royal Velvet' and 'Ruby Glow'. These are all very compact in their growth and flowering habit and produce their main flowering flush in late spring or

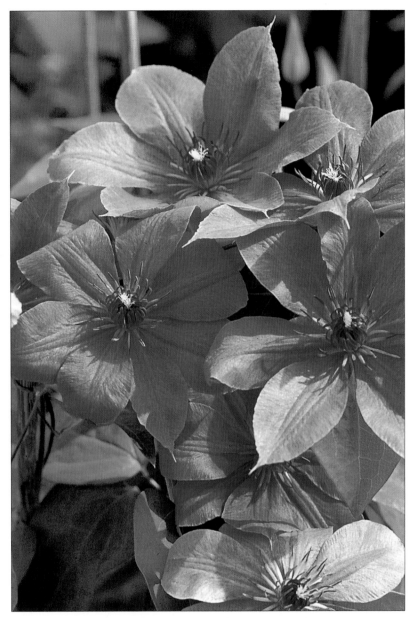

'Ruby Glow' has a compact, free flowering habit, ideal for container growing.

early summer. They are ideal to train and make an absolutely glorious, if perhaps oversized, pot plant for a small area, producing twenty to thirty flowers on a plant only 1m high in a container with a 30–45cm diameter. The slightly later-flowering types in this group are perhaps the most rewarding. Varieties similar to 'Nelly Moser' and 'The President', which flower during early summer, are also followed by a further crop of flowers during the late

summer months.

The *montana* group and some of the vigorous, tall-growing species such as *tangutica*, *tibetana*, *serratifolia* and *rehderiana* are, unfortunately, far too vigorous to be grown in a container successfully.

Flowering of these types would be rewarding during the first few years when the compost in the container is fresh and contains the correct balance of foods; but when top growth reaches five to seven metres and the root system more or less fills the container, the gardener would be forever watering and feeding the plant.

The late-flowering, large-flowered cultivars can be grown successfully although they do not make the same type of compact plant as the early large-flowered group. This group, which includes the famous *Clematis x jackmanii* and its many forms, flowers on the new growth only; therefore, all the previous season's top growth is removed in the early spring allowing new growth to be made. This new growth needs careful training and one should remember that the flowers are produced at the end of each stem generally after two-and-a-half metres of growth has been accomplished. Despite the additional work involved, this group, plus the small flowered cultivars of the *viticella group*, are worth the extra effort of container growing.

Choosing and preparing your container

The material from which the container is made is important. The use of plastic tubs or plastic containers should be avoided, the main reason being that the container does not insulate the clematis roots from the heat of summer or from the cold of winter. As mentioned earlier in the book, clematis prefer a cool root run and, therefore, a plant growing in a thin walled plastic tub in an exposed sunny situation would be caused great distress in a hot summer, even with extra watering. In winter, such a container would again expose the clematis root system to very little or almost no insulation against severe frosts. However, there is still a great range of containers to choose from: for example, old half beer barrels, stone, earthenware or some of the more pleasant, modern designed wooden containers.

The size of the container is, however, important. It should be not less than 45cm deep with a diameter of 30–40cm, larger if available, and there should be sufficient drainage holes. With a container of this size there should be at least three drainage holes, each with a 5cm diameter, or five to six holes with a 2cm diameter.

Pebbles or broken pottery must be placed over the drainage holes to a depth of about 6cm; small stones and pea gravel scattered over the pebbles will also assist drainage and avoid the clogging of the holes with compost after watering, or by earth-worms. Make sure that if the bottom surface of the container sits flat on the standing area, stones are placed underneath the container to lift it off the ground: this will greatly assist drainage and avoid blockage and water saturation of the container during prolonged rain or snow periods in the winter months.

'Fujimusume' is a must for a container on the patio.

1. Canes tied wigwam fashion to provide support for clematis
2. Root crown buried 6–8cm below soil surface
3. Soil surface covered with low growing plants providing shade for root system
4. Main base roots slightly loosened
5. John Innes Potting Compost No.3
6. Layer of small stones or pea gravel to assist drainage
7. Pebbles or broken pottery placed over drainage holes to a depth of 6cm
8. Container raised off ground to prevent drainage holes blocking

Planting and training your container grown clematis

CLEMATIS SUITABLE FOR CONTAINER CULTURE:

Winter flowering or early spring under glass:
(glasshouse or conservatory conditions)
afoliata
australis
cirrhosa
cirrhosa balearica
cirrhosa 'Freckles'
florida Alba Plena
florida 'Sieboldii'
forsteri
gentianoides
paniculata

April flowering:
alpina 'Columbine'
alpina 'Constance'
alpina 'Frankie'
alpina 'Helsingborg'
alpina 'Pamela Jackman'
alpina 'Pink Flamingo'
alpina 'Tage Lundell'
alpina 'White Columbine'
macropetala
macropetala 'Floralia'
macropetala 'Jan Lindmark'
macropetala 'Lagoon'
macropetala 'Markham's Pink'

Early May flowering
'Anna Louise'
'Asao'
'Barbara Dibley'
'Bees Jubilee'
'Burma Star'
'Corona'

'Dawn'
'Edith'
'Elsa Späth'
'Fireworks'
'Guernsey Cream'
'Haku Ookan'
'H.F. Young'
'Horn of Plenty'
'Lady Londesborough'
'Liberation'
'Masquerade'
'Miss Bateman'
'Moonlight'
'Mrs P.B. Truax'
'Pink Champagne' (Kakio)
'Royal Velvet'
'Ruby Glow'
'Scartho Gem'
'Souvenir de Capitain Thuilleaux'

End May/early June flowering
'Arctic Queen'
'Barbara Jackman'
'Countess of Lovelace'
'Daniel Deronda'
'Duchess of Edinburgh'
'Dr. Ruppel'
florida 'Alba Plena'
florida 'Sieboldii'
'John Warren'
'Kathleen Wheeler'
'Lady Northcliffe'
'Lasurstern'
'Lord Nevill'
'Marie Boisselot'
'Mrs. Cholmondeley'
'Mrs. George Jackman'

'Mrs. N. Thompson'
'Multi Blue'
'Nelly Moser'
'Niobe'
'Proteus'
'Richard Pennell'
'Rouge Cardinal'
'Royalty'
'Silver Moon'
'The President'
'Vyvyan Pennell'
'William Kennett'

Late June/July onwards flowering
'Cardinal Wyszynski'
'Comtesse de Bouchaud'
'Dorothy Walton'
'General Sikorski'
'Hagley Hybrid'
'John Huxtable'
'Perrins Pride'
'Petit Faucon'
'Rhapsody'
'Serenata'
'Sunset'
viticella 'Abundance'
viticella 'Alba Luxurians'
viticella 'Betty Corning'
viticella 'Etoile Violette'
viticella 'Kermesina'
viticella 'Mme Julia Correvon'
viticella 'Purpurea Plena Elegans'
viticella 'Royal Velours'
viticella 'Venosa Violacea'

In my experience, the only suitable compost to put into the container is that prepared under the John Innes formula, and John Innes potting soil No. 3 should be used. The No. 3 mixture is of extra strength, Nos. 1 and 2 being far too weak for long-term pot culture. This compost is readily available from many garden centres and garden shops. There are many other composts offered for sale, including loam-free mixtures which contain a percentage of peat and grit or sand. They are most useful for short-term growing of crops, especially annuals, but are of no use for long-term pot culture where they require far too much attention to maintain a correct nutrient balance and where liquid feeding also becomes difficult if the compost dries out. When using John Innes potting compost, the top 6–8cm of soil should be carefully replaced each spring using the same John Innes No. 3 potting compost. At this time, attention should also be paid to the drainage holes, ensuring they are not blocked.

Planting your container

After the correct choice of clematis has been made, a suitable container prepared and filled to within 6cm of the rim, planting may now commence. Planting in a container is, or can be described as, re-potting and may be carried out at any time of the year, although obviously the points mentioned under the section dealing with garden planting should still be considered. Summer planted clematis will require more watering in order to achieve good and quick root establishment.

The plant, still in its original pot, should be plunged into a bucket of water and left to soak for at least 15 to 20 minutes. Then carefully remove the pot from the root ball, loosening the outer, bottom-most roots slightly, as previously described on page 18. Bury the root crown at least 6–8cm below the soil surface of the container as this will help the plant's survival rate if damage should occur at any stage in the plant's lifetime by animals, or when pruning or re-potting is being carried out.

In exposed, cold locations where heavy snowfalls or wet winters can be expected or, even worse, where low temperatures can be expected without snow cover, then it is advisable to take clematis growing in containers into a well-lit garage or out-building. This will avoid the root system being exposed unnecessarily to severe conditions and will prevent it from being damaged by long periods of severe frost or becoming sodden with water. This will also avoid damage to the ripened top growth from the previous growing season, as one needs to retain as much as possible to attain the largest possible amount of flower for the next flowering season. My friends in northern parts of the U.S.A., Canada and Northern Europe take their container-grown clematis under cover each winter so they can achieve a good, well clothed flowering plant for the following spring. If this has to be done, then obviously it is important that any clematis grown in a container should have its support attached to the container or be supported by a frame which is anchored into the compost: it would become a

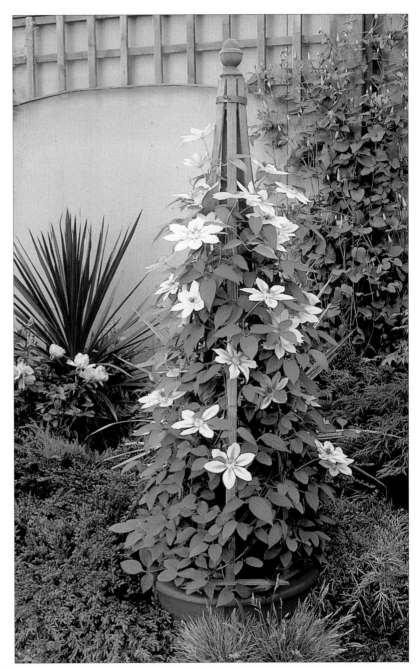

Here Clematis 'Nelly Moser' has been trained to practically cover its support.

little difficult to remove part of the house wall each autumn to take inside with the clematis attched!

Pruning and training the container-grown clematis

Pruning and training of a pot or container-grown clematis follows the same basic principles as for a free-growing plant, but careful pruning and training are more important if the best looking container plant is to be produced. The first spring after planting (depending on weather conditions), the clematis must be pruned hard with all stems previously produced being removed down to 24cm above soil level. This severe action is necessary

Careful pruning and training are important to encourage a bushy plant. Depending on weather conditions, the first spring after planting is the time to prune hard, reducing stems to 24cm above soil level. Prune above the newly formed leaf axil buds to encourage lots of new growth and as this appears tie it in horizontally onto the supports.

to encourage several new stems to be produced at a low level, thus forming the basic framework of the plant for the future.

The pruning cut should be made just above a strong leaf axil bud, or better still, a pair of buds. These buds will be visible during early spring. When new growth commences and three pairs of leaves or nodes have been formed, the growing tip must then be removed. This will encourage the production of two or three new shoots from each stem, at the stage when the new growth is still soft and green and before the unapparent leaf axil buds have become at all woody.

The new growth subsequently produced should be carefully trained and tied into position on to the various supports that have been provided (more about the choice of supports later). If possible, train the stems to grow almost horizontally in a circular manner around the support framework, commencing as low as you can.

After the hard work in the spring, no further pruning is required until the following year and you may allow your clematis the freedom of flowering. I assure you, if you have been strong-minded enough to carry out this pruning the first spring after planting, you will be justly rewarded. The many plants which I have prepared for our exhibits at recent Chelsea Flower Shows were all treated in this way.

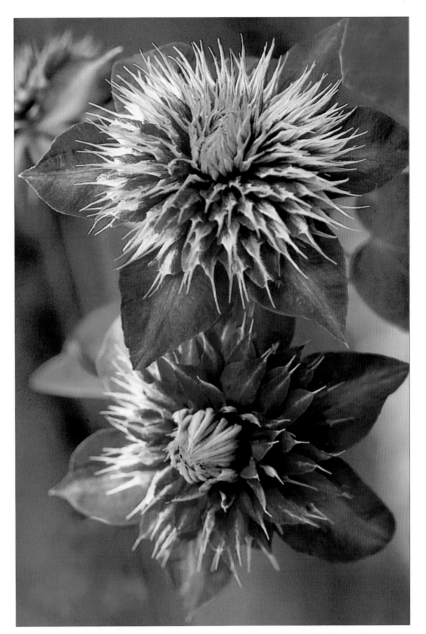

This free flowering, compact, double clematis 'Multi Blue' makes it ideal for container growing.

Support

The selection of a support or framework for the container grown clematis needs consideration. If the clematis is to be grown against a wall or through another host plant, then the support is already decided, but an auxiliary cane should be led from the container to the main support or strong branch of the host. For the free-standing container plant there are many and varied metal and wooden supports for plants available on the market. Simple cane or stick supports may also be placed inside the container and tied together at the top, wigwam fashion. Metal rods coated with a polythene or plastic film and bent into various hoops or pyramid shapes are all equally interesting and worthy of experiment. The climbing supports made of wood and shown on page 50 are very useful clematis supports, this particular one is called a Flower Belle.

Looking after your container grown clematis

Throughout the growing season, from spring until late summer, container-grown clematis will need regular attention such as the tying-in of new growth. It is essential that the new growth is tied in as it is produced and this will only take a few minutes per week.

Watering is the most time consuming job, with each 45cm clematis container requiring the equivalent of a gallon (4.5 litres) per day during the dry spring and summer weather. A guide to water requirement can be tested by disturbing the compost a few centimetres below the surface. If it is moist or sticks to the finger, the plant will not require water on that day; but if the compost is like dust, then water is necessary. Do not give the plant small amounts of water at a time since this will only keep the surface moist and the area where the roots are at the bottom of the container will remain dry. If watering is restricted, this will reduce the top growth, which will in turn limit the number of flowers produced. It is most important to remember that sufficient water is a must with the cultivars which are expected to carry a second batch of flowers during mid summer. Basically, watering reaches a peak during mid-summer when water will be required each day, unless there has been rain. Less water will be required as autumn approaches and stopped altogether by the mid autumn, except for the very occasional watering necessary to stop the soil from becoming dust dry. Liquid fertilizer can be incorporated during watering but should never be applied to dry soil: water first and then use. If liquid feed is taken up by roots which have been starved of water, the root hairs will be damaged causing unwanted harm to your clematis. There are many liquid feeds offered on the market and any reliable brand-name product is suitable. A well balanced feed with equal parts of Nitrogen and Potash is best for the growing season. As previously mentioned in the section dealing with "Annual Feeding and Mulching of Established Plants" (page 20), the liquid feeding of container-grown clematis should also stop prior to flowering. It is therefore advisable to stop feeding as soon as the most prominent flower bud is about the size of a pea. The continuation of

Canes tied wigwam fashion are the easiest framework to make to encourage the clematis to climb upwards.

clear water is vital and, in fact, should be attended to very closely. If the container-grown plant should become at all dry at this time, the successful flowering of the plant could be in severe doubt.

As soon as the last flowers fade away, the use of liquid feed becomes very important again so that healthy new growth can be made to produce the next crop of flowers in the season. Liquid feeding should be discontinued by late summer because the amount of new growth made from that time will be naturally reduced and it is important that growth should be hardened and ripened for the following season, especially with the early-flowering cultivars which flower on the previous season's ripened stems.

Pruning in subsequent years

When all foliage has died, and possibly fallen to the ground during the winter, and the fat leaf axil buds are visible during the later winter months and early spring, pruning and training can commence.

All varieties which flower before early summer belonging to Group One and Two should be carefully pruned. The amount of pruning required must be judged by experience. However, as a guide to the beginner, all dead and weak stems should be reduced to the point where strong, swollen leaf axil buds are present. The "fat" buds are the ones which will produce the first large flowers during late spring and early summer. The selected stems that remain after pruning should be tied into place and great care must be taken not to knock off any buds or crack any of the stems as they are being trained. The exact position in which the stems are tied must be left to the gardener and the individual framework that is being used. However, if the stems are tied in an almost horizontal position, new growth will be produced and grow vertically, giving a good cover to the lower part of the supports. The stems of the large-flowered cultivars should be spaced far enough from each other so that each swollen leaf axil bud will develop and hopefully produce a flower which will have sufficient space to grow without overcrowding. The decision as to how many stems to leave or remove will be made easier by experience. It is easy to be greedy and leave too many stems which will cause reduced flower size.

If the later-flowering types are being used, the pruning for this is the same as for the open ground or garden varieties of the same group: simply remove all top growth down to just above the swollen buds, which normally are in the vicinity of the base of the previous season's growth. As new growth appears, this should be tied into position before it becomes over 30cm long. These stems also can be trained in a semi-horizontal position. If this growth is merely allowed to grow straight to the top of the support, the plant will look less interesting and you will be disappointed with the result.

The pruning and training sounds most complicated when written in this manner but do not be put off container-grown clematis. Admittedly the work is time consuming, but it is definitely worth the effort and time taken. The cold fingers experienced during the winter and early spring months, the backache etc., will be truly rewarded when the plants are in full flower, and the pain will be forgotten.

With experience gained over two or three years, the enthusiastic gardener will soon start to experiment with different varieties to grow, or the shapes and style of framework used, and many fine "pot plants" will be produced for the conservatory, garden room, patio or balcony.

CLEMATIS IN THE CONSERVATORY

If a conservatory, garden room or cold glasshouse is available, a succession of flowering "pot plants" may be produced by careful selection of species, their forms and cultivars. These can be forced or retarded and brought into this extended garden or living-room. In Victorian times, the culture of clematis in this way for the house, conservatory or show bench was well practised. Today, we have an even larger selection to choose from which includes the slightly tender evergreen types that will provide foliage and flower during the winter months. The range of cultivars being raised by crossing some of the New Zealand species is to be looked out for. *x cartmanii* 'Joe' is one which produces a dense mat of

CLEMATIS FOR THE CONSERVATORY

alpina 'Columbine'
alpina 'Constance'
alpina 'Frankie'
alpina 'Pink Flamingo'
'Anna Louise'
'Arctic Queen'
'Asao'
australis
'Bees Jubilee'
'Burma Star'
x cartmanii 'Joe'
cirrhosa balearica
cirrhosa 'Freckles'
'Daniel Deronda'
'Dawn'
florida 'Alba Plena'
florida 'Sieboldii'
forsteri
'Guernsey Cream'
'Lady Londesborough'
'Lasurstern'
macropetala 'Markhams Pink'
'Masquerade'
'Miss Bateman'
'Multi Blue'
'Nelly Moser'
'Niobe'
paniculata
'Petit Faucon'
'Pink Champagne'
'Rhapsody'
'Royal Velvet'
'Royalty'
'Ruby Glow'
'The President'
viticella 'Betty Corning'
viticella 'Madame Julia Correvon'
viticella 'Venosa Violacea'
'Vyvyan Pennell'

white flowers a little over an inch wide. As I write this section I have a plant in my office in a 3 litre pot of this outstanding clematis on a 60cm high wire, dome-shaped frame, it has over 400 flowers !!! and has been flowering already for two weeks with another two weeks I guess to flower, the plant would last even longer in cooler room or glasshouse. However, ones that are more readily available at present are the good forms of the charming *C. cirrhosa*, *cirrhosa balearica* with finely cut slightly bronze foliage, and the new *cirrhosa* 'Freckles', a plant I introduced in 1989. *C. cirrhosa* 'Freckles' has the largest flowers of any of the cirrhosa forms; the leaves, too, are larger than the form. The foliage of all these plants is evergreen.

The flowers of 'Freckles' are borne from the ripened previous season's stems during late autumn and early winter, with the occasional summer flower. The flowers of all *cirrhosa* types are nodding and comprise of four tepals. They are cream inside and are covered in pink-red blotches. *C. cirrhosa* 'Freckles' has flowers 4–5cm in depth which are slightly scented. The tepals recurve a little at the edges, revealing the stunning colour inside the flower. Its flowers have the most intense colour and are almost totally covered with blotches. The other forms of *cirrhosa* flower from just after Christmas under glass.

Two good New Zealand clematis to look out for are *C. paniculata*, with white tepals, and *C. forsteri*. The flowers of paniculata are produced, as with all winter-flowering clematis, from the previous season's ripened stems. This species varies; therefore, a good broad flowered form should be selected. The best have flowers 4–5cm across with lovely pink anthers, which are produced in late winter. As mentioned in an earlier chapter, the best winter-flowering clematis for strong scent is *C. forsteri* which has creamy-green small flowers which are produced in great abundance. When this plant is in full flower in late winter or early spring, the lemon verbena scent from the flowers is almost overpowering. *C. australis* is similar but has more finely cut foliage which is most attractive but has not so strong a scent.

The winter-flowering, small-flowered clematis can be followed by the

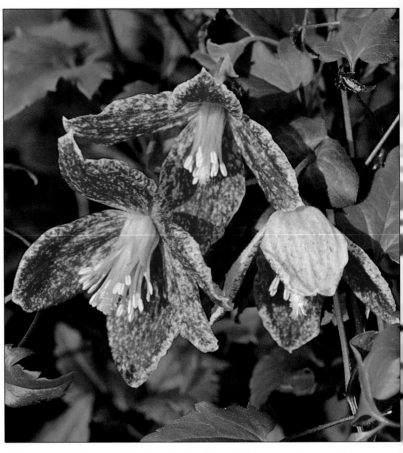

The evergreen Clematis cirrhosa 'Freckles' will provide foliage and flowers in the conservatory during the winter months.

earliest of the early, large-flowered cultivars which would flower during early spring under cold glasshouse conditions. Again, these produce their flowers from the ripened previous season's stems. Some of the earliest to flower are 'Asao' pale pink, 'Pink Champagne' deep pink-mauve, 'Dawn' very delicate pale pink, 'Miss Bateman' white with red anthers, 'Wada's Primrose' cream and 'Lady Londesborough' pale blue. These early, large-flowered cultivars are sometimes flowering just before the charming, nodding *aquilegia*, or Granny's Bonnet, like *alpina* and *macropetala* types. The *alpinas* have single flowers with four tepals and come in shades of blue, white, red and mauve. The macropetalas have double flowers and are available in similar shades. Some of the freest flowering *alpina* types are *alpina* 'Colum-

bine', 'White Columbine', 'Helsingborg', 'Frankie', 'Constance' and 'Pink Flamingo' . Some of the outstanding *macropetala* types are *macropetala* the species, 'Markham's Pink', 'Jan Lindmark' and 'White Moth'.

The next main flowering batch are the slightly later, large-flowered cultivars such as 'Nelly Moser' pink striped, 'The President' deep purple-blue, 'Lasurstern' blue, 'Bees Jubilee' pink striped, 'Niobe' deep red, 'Horn of Plenty' mauve, 'Guernsey Cream' cream and 'Fireworks' a new stunning mauve-blue with red stripes, of more recent introduction are 'Anna Louise' petunia-red with contrasting purple/red bars, 'Royal Velvet' reddish velvet and 'Masquerade' lavender blue. The doubles such as 'Royalty' and 'Vyvyan Pennell' both mauve-purple, 'Proteus' mauve-pink, 'Arctic Queen' white

Clematis x cartmanii 'Joe' produces a dense mat of flowers.

the flower colour may change slightly, due to lower light levels, but they are still worthy of time and effort and give much added interest late in the autumn months.

Before I conclude this section I must mention—or rave about—the extraordinary long-flowering duo of *C. florida* 'Sieboldii' and its double white form, 'Alba Plena'. Given good growing conditions in a container, these two (which were introduced from Japan as long ago as 1837) will flower almost continuously from March to December when growing under glasshouse conditions in England while in Guernsey in our glasshouse they are hardly ever out of flower. They are not so rampant as the large-flowered cultivars but are most colourful. *C. florida* 'Sieboldii' has creamy white tepals and a stunning purple boss of petaloid stamens; the flowers can be up to 8cm across and are produced in great abundance. 'Alba Plena' has a fully double white flower, about the same size. As light levels decrease, the white tepals become more creamy-green in colour and, by December, become almost green in normal, cold glasshouse conditions.

As you will have realised by now, it is possible to grow clematis in containers and have them flowering throughout the year in a conservatory, garden room or cold glasshouse, if careful selection is given to cultivation and the selection of species or cultivars.

'Daniel Deronda' semi-double, purple-blue can all be used to extend the early part of the summer. Any of the above mentioned types, except the evergreens, can either be forced on by using a little extra gentle heat or be retarded by placing the plants in a shaded north-facing position, out of direct sunshine.

Some of the newer introductions that are also proving their worth for both spring/summer and repeat flowering in the autumn are 'Sunset' deep scarlet red, 'Liberation' reddish pink and the pink striped 'Sugar Candy'.

The later-flowering *x jackmanii* types, such as 'Comtesse de Bouchaud' pink, 'John Huxtable' white, 'Hagley Hybrid' pink-mauve or the free-flowering *viticella* cultivars, such as 'Etoile Violette' purple, 'Madame Julia Correvon' red, 'Alba Luxurians' white with green tips to the tepals, 'Polish Spirit' purple and 'Venosa Violacea' white with purple veining can be used and respond to forcing. The middle season large-flowered cultivars such as 'Marie Boisselot' white, 'Will Goodwin' pale blue and 'W E Gladstone' blue, are almost a little too vigorous to grow in a container for the conservatory; however, if enough space exists and a container up to 60/70cm diameter with a depth of 60 cm can be used, and a 150 cm high trellis can be supported by the container, then these extra large-flowered cultivars can be used to flower from early summer until early winter. The flowers may become smaller as the season continues and

Clematis on Walls and Other Structures

Clematis are useful plants to grace a wide range of structures. Some vigorous types are most successful for covering unsightly walls, while others can be used to give additional interest and colour to other plants and climbers growing over pergolas, archways and fences.

Walls

You will have gathered, by now, that I prefer plants to grow in a natural situation, as far as possible. The placing of a clematis plant to grow against a blank wall goes very much against my way of gardening. However, I accept the point that in some cases this may be necessary and must be done.

If a clematis is to be grown against a wall there are a few important things to remember. Firstly, the soil preparation should be good and the plant should be positioned at least 30cm away from the base of the wall, as shown in the diagram on page 14. Secondly, the plant should be pruned hard in its first two years to encourage it to produce a good low framework of branches and the stems may be trained in horizontal manner and then allowed to grow upwards. This pruning and training early in the plant's life will provide a wellformed

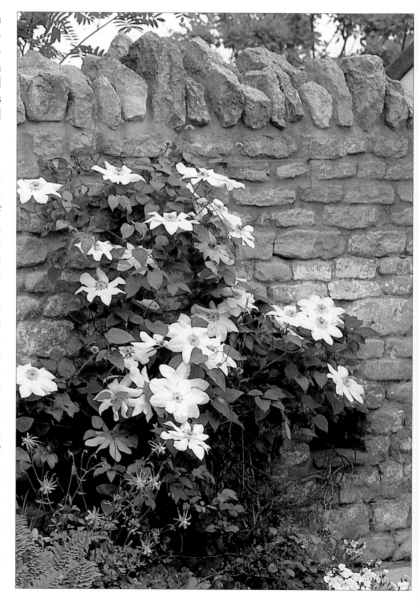

The bright, white flowers of 'Henryi' stand out against this stone wall.

plant and avoid that all too familiar sight of one straight clematis stem and then a bird's nest collection of growth about two metres above ground level.

Several factors will influence the choice of plant: the area which is to be covered, the ultimate height which the clematis may reach, and the flower colour in relation to the colour of the background, avoiding, for example, pale flower colours on sunny, south walls. The shading of the clematis root system and lower part of the plant is a must on a dry, sunny, south or south-west facing wall. The use of low growing shrubs such as lavenders, helianthemums, hebes, heather etc., will give the necessary shade to the root systems.

Artificial supports

The selection of support must be given thought and there are numerous types of trellis and plastic-covered wire available in various shapes, sizes and colours. The choice must be left to the gardener to select the one most in keeping with the wall or style of house. The total height and weight of the clematis foliage which the support will have to carry must also be taken into account. On outbuildings ordinary 7cm wide mesh chicken wire or sheep netting for the vigorous species is practical, but this would not be the case if the site were adjacent to an important door entrance.

The clematis vines need to be able to reach a support in one form or another every 8–10cm, either horizontally or vertically; and to bridge the gap between soil level and the first strong support, a cane should be firmly attached to the wall support and the first growths of the clematis tied to the cane.

Using wall-trained shrubs as supports

The use of a wall-trained shrub has many advantages because the framework of the host branches or stems allows the clematis to grow naturally and very little training is necessary. Obviously the host needs to be tied against the wall but elaborate trellis and wire supports are unnecessary as most wall trained shrubs can be tied to a masonry nail placed into the wall at the required spacings. Most host plants should be given two years to become established before a clematis is planted to grow through them.

The choice of host seems almost endless but some of the most satisfactory are the evergreens including *Azara*, *Camellia*, *Ceanothus*, *Garrya elliptica*, *Magnolia grandiflora* and *Pyracantha*. Deciduous shrubs such as jasmine, *Wisteria*, *Buddleia*, *Chaenomeles*, roses, *Cotoneaster horizontalis*, *Cytisus battandieri*, etc., also give sufficient support.

The selection of host and clematis is an easy one and the possible combinations are extensive. The clematis can be chosen to flower at the same time, or before, or after its host. All of

The bareness of this wall is contrasted by the abundance of flowers from this Clematis viticella 'Purpurea Plena Elegans'.
(Photographed by the author in a garden in Estonia)

Clematis on Walls and Other Structures

Clematis alpina 'Ruby' is providing cover for this old brick shed wall.

Clematis on Walls and Other Structures

the less vigorous species and all of the large-flowered cultivars whether early, mid or late season flowering, may be used.

The clematis that need the support of wall trained shrubs include the evergreen, early-flowering species and their cultivars that produce the gigantic-sized flowers. They dislike a windy position and need the protection of a wall site, as do some of the less vigorous species, for instance *florida* 'Sieboldii' and *florida* 'Alba Plena'. On a north facing wall the *alpina* and *macropetala* types look delightful when growing through *Chaenomeles*. 'Nelly Moser', 'Dawn', 'Bees Jubilee' and 'Lincoln Star', with their flowers in various shades of pink, brighten up a north-facing wall and look well when grown through camellias or pyracanthas.

Climbing and wall-trained roses give the clematis vines plenty of support when climbing through their branching stems. Here, the choice of clematis and rose is important so that the pruning requirements of the rose and clematis will be basically the same. Life can be very difficult for the clematis stems and damage may be caused if the rose needs severe pruning annually and the clematis does not, but this can be avoided with a little thought. The point made in the last sentence obviously applies to all of the other wall shrubs used. Thought must also be given to the ultimate height of both clematis and host: to grow a *montana* or *tangutica* over a *Ceanothus* or *Pyracantha* would mean suffocation for the unfortunate host within four years.

Posts

The thought of using a clematis to clothe an individual bare post hurts me about as much as planting a clematis to grow against a blank wall. If posts are in need of being furnished with a shrub, I believe that both for appearance's sake and for the plant's well-being a clematis grown in association with another shrub, such as a pillar or climbing rose, makes a far better proposition.

If, however, space is only available for a clematis, some varieties are better than others. The late-flowering, large-flowered cultivars are best. 'Hagley Hybrid' which produces masses of pink flowers from July onwards, and 'Madame Edouard André' with her dusky-red flowers, also from July onwards, may be used alone to give a colourful display. Of the slightly newer clematis, two Polish cultivars, 'Niobe' and 'General Sikorski', are also most useful for this purpose, both being vigorous and free-flowering. 'Niobe' has very deep red flowers with contrasting yellow anthers, and 'General Sikorski' has large rounded mid-blue flowers with creamy centres.

If a more rampageous clematis is required, the *montana* types or the late-flowering species such as *tangutica* and *tibetana*, with their yellow lantern-like flowers, may be used; but they will need more attention, especially when they are in full flower and foliage. The stems will need tying-in to avoid damage during any strong winds or gales, and the supporting post will need to be of a hardwood with the bottom sunk at least 65cm into the soil and also firmly anchored in a concrete base. Three slightly less vigorous clematis from the *tibetana* group, that can also be grown up posts, are *tibetana* ssp. *vernayi* 'Ludlow and Sheriff' with thick tepals and delicately cut glaucous foliage, *glauca akebioides* (described earlier) which also has attractive glaucous foliage and is covered in

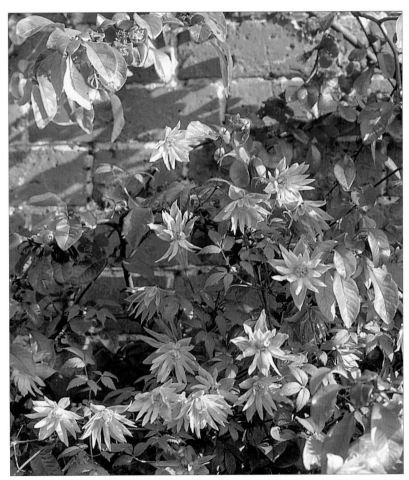

Clematis macropetala is growing here on a north wall with the support of Chaenomeles.

Clematis potanini var. 'Fargesii' gracefully clothes this bare post.

Lonicera (honeysuckle), Wisteria, Akebia, Actinidia, Ampelopsis, Chaenomeles, Hedera (ivy), Jasminum, Parthenocissus (virginia creeper) Passiflora and Vitis (the ornamental and fruiting vines) all give a great variation of flower, foliage and form which is complemented by the clematis.

The *montana* family may be used on a large pergola or archway, and the stems and foliage will eventually give a great deal of cover and shade on the top of the framework. The flowers will generally be near the growing tip of the plants (from the previous season's ripened stems). The supports and posts of the pergola will also need clothing and the *alpina*, *macropetala* and early large-flowered cultivars will fulfil this role, producing their flowers from late spring until early summer. The mid-season and late large-flowered cultivars will give flowers from early summer onwards and also give more height with growth reaching the top of the support posts at two-and-a-half metres and then trailing along to the top to cascade back down again covered in flowers. Hopefully, the large-flowered cultivars will also give a second crop of flowers during late summer and early autumn. The planning needs careful thought so that the archway or pergola does not become too heavily leaden with foliage, causing structural damage: stout support posts and rigid cross bars should be used.

The pruning requirements of both host and clematis must also be observed. If any of the early large-flowered clematis are used because of the choice of colour, they may be pruned hard; the early large flowers would be fewer but a crop of flowers would be produced on the new growth six weeks or so later than normal.

The kinking and twisting of stems, when handling, pruning, or training other shrubs on the framework, should be avoided if at all possible, as they may cause partial damage to the vine

a mass of small flowers which are bronze-yellow on the back of the tepal, and *graveolens* 'Gravetye Variety' which is a good, fresh green foliaged orientalis type with nicely cut foliage and deep creamy yellow flowers.

Pergolas and archways
Rustic pergolas and archways add charm and character to any garden and offer yet another place where the enthusiastic clematis grower may cultivate and grow a range of clematis. A pergola or archway given over entirely to clematis is not to be desired; but if other climbers and shrubs are used in association with clematis then the effect is tremendous, giving colour, flower and foliage for most months of the year. Climbing and pillar roses,

Clematis on Walls and Other Structures

The deep purple-blue flowers of 'Daniel Deronda' climb through a wall-trained robinia.

later in the year when the foliage and flowers need every bit of moisture and sap the stems can provide. Clematis of different varieties but similar flowering period may be grown together but it is advisable to choose plants with the same pruning requirements. Life becomes increasingly tedious if one attempts to disentangle the growth and stems of a *montana* and a late large-flowered cultivar from one another during pruning. One's fingers become cold, one's temper is tested, one's eyes become rather crossed and the clematis stems become damaged. Unless you are even-tempered and have good eyesight, be warned!

Fences

A fence made of chain-link, wire, or wood is one of the coldest places to ask any self-respecting plant to grow through or over. Therefore, only the strong-growing species or small-flowered cultivar clematis can be considered. The height of the fence is not important since a clematis will climb until there is no further vertical support, at which point its vines will fall back naturally. So if the fence is one or even three metres in height, the choice of clematis is left open between the strong-growing types.

The *alpina* and *macropetala*, the *montanas* and the *viticella* cultivars, coupled with the robust-growing, late-flowering species such as *tangutica, tibetana, serratifolia* and *potanini* var. 'Fargesii' will all tackle the job and succeed. A selection from these clematis will give a good continuity of flowers throughout the season. One point to remember—if the fence is only one metre high, a *montana* or *tangutica* can each cover such a fence to the length of at least eight to nine metres after about three to four years. A selection of *alpina* types and the *viticella* cultivars would be best for a low, one-metre-high fence giving flower from spring until early autumn, with the exception of a few weeks during early summer. The use of a *montana* cultivar on a low wall, possibly alongside a set of garden steps, in association with a variegated-leafed ivy (*Hedera*) will make a colourful addition to any garden.

Growing Clematis in North America

Having decided with my publisher and my editor that in the third edition of my book a chapter should be devoted to the growing of clematis in North America, I asked my friends in these countries if they thought this would be useful. The resounding reply was "yes"—'*provide the information that is available*'—'*in some states due to the extremely variable climatic zones so little information is available*'. Having decided to go ahead I could see the obvious additional benefits that would become available to other growers of clematis throughout the world, especially if I introduced winter hardiness zones. Therefore my approach to this chapter has been more about climatic conditions than other cultural details as these are generally covered in other chapters within the book. However, wherever I have been able to pick up any useful tips that will help with species or cultivar selections and cultural advice this is included.

While on a flight to New York in June 1995 I took along with me Ernest Markham's book entitled 'Clematis', as I knew there was a chapter devoted to the growing of clematis in North America, hoping this would give me inspiration and perhaps some guidelines for this chapter. The book first published in 1935 some 60 years ago has a marvellous chapter written by J E Spingarn, who was described by Ernest Markham as 'the well known writer and grower of these climbers on the other side of the Atlantic'. The first and second editions of Making the Most of Clematis have sold very well in North America for many years, so I therefore read with some amusement and a little frustration the following words from Mr Spingarn's chapter 'Clematis in North America':

'*The conditions that surround gardening in England are so different from those in the United States and Canada, in climate and soil, in plant diseases and insect pests, and in many other ways, that English garden books are seldom of much practical use to the American Gardener. It is this reason that Mr Markham has asked me to contribute a brief chapter on clematis in America: every English garden book should have an American appendix of some sort if it is intended to be read by American as well as English gardeners.*'

Sadly it has taken me nearly twenty years since the first edition of this book was published to reach the same conclusions!!!

Having read the Spingarn chapter with interest I discovered that in many respects the attitude to growing clematis in these two countries has

'Sugar Candy', this new cultivar will be successful when planted in hardiness zones 4–6.

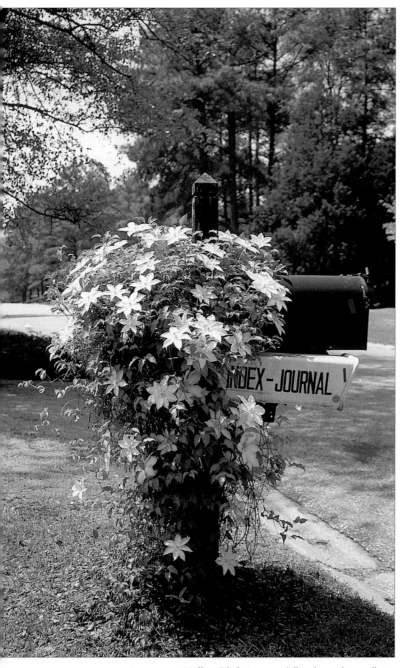

'Gillian Blades' successfully adorns this mailbox.

for these trials to provide helpful information. So therefore the problem is still with me of how to provide a chapter that will be of use to gardeners in the very, very variable climate zones. However I have been fortunate to be able to gather information based upon lecture talks that I have given in these areas and more recently by attending the San Francisco Landscape Garden Show where I was able to gain first hand information from the public.

Historically only certain varieties have been growing in certain areas or states as these have been the only ones available, and consequently have wrongly been thought to be the only clematis that would 'survive' or 'do well' in these areas and the lack of evaluation trials have not dispelled this theory.

Mr Spingarn's records and knowledge and that which I have gained in recent years seem to vary very little and he quotes a list of these varieties that will 'do well' or 'survive' given the extreme heat and cold. I feel it is worth my repeating some of his helpful comments as I believe them to be firm guidelines of what species and cultivars can or are already established in these harsh climates. His conclusion that he drew over sixty years ago—that Americans had been slow to use their own native species in their gardens has been confirmed by my own findings and those of Mr John Elsley from South Carolina, who is respected throughout North America as one of their leading plantsmen. Mr Spingarn points out that there are a dozen native species that are worthy of a place in gardens. He noted that *Clematis texensis*, a native of Texas, has been found to be hardy in New York and New England and that it has flowered in Bar Habour and in Ottawa. Sadly 'true' or good forms of this species are not readily available either in Europe or North America. However one of its cultivars *C. texensis* 'Duchess of Albany' a great favourite

changed very little until very recently. Certainly the selection of species and cultivars offered today with a few exceptions are still limited to the few tried and tested from 60 years ago. However, in the last four to five years some leading nurserymen and mail order companies have extended their list of clematis offered for sale.

I have been able to exchange clematis with north American nurserymen and gardeners and recently I have been able to send clematis collections to various botanical gardens in both the United States and Canada for evaluation purposes. Obviously a few more years, a dry summer and a few more very cold winters are needed of mine proved to be winter hardy in Ontario during the winter of 1993/94 when it recovered and grew after temperatures of –30°F. C. crispa was also noted by Mr Spingarn as being 'hardy almost anywhere'. This charming species which is a native of the southern states varies in colour a little from pale blue to white and has recurving tips to its tepals. One of the more recent clematis introduced in north America is viticella 'Betty Corning' which is believed to be a cross between C. crispa and C. viticella. C. viticella, a European species introduced into north America in the early part of the nineteenth century, has proved to be winter hardy, to at least –30°F, ninety miles north of New York. Therefore it is hoped that C. viticella 'Betty Corning' will have retained the hardiness of its two parents. It has certainly proved successful in Southern Carolina in the heat and humidity where I saw it producing its second crop of flowers in early June 1995.

Other North American species that Mr Spingarn noted that I know are generally available and natives of the east are: C. pitcheri, C. reticulata, C. verticillans, C. versicolor, C. viorna and the vigorous C. ligusticifolia and from the western states C. columbiana (now known as C. grosserata).

Other species which were introduced into North America before 1935 such as C. heracleifolia davidiana, C. potanini var. 'Fargesii', C. integrifolia, C. x jouiniana, C. orientalis, C. serratifolia, C. tangutica, C. terniflora (formerly known as C. paniculata) and C. vitalba and C. viticella have all proved to be winter hardy to –30°F ninety miles north of New York.

Mr Spingarn also points out that Dr F Skinner from Dropmore, Manitoba—where temperatures drop to –40°F and occasionally to –60°F had been successful in flowering the following more readily available species: aethusifolia, alpina, alpina sibirica, brevicaudata, douglasii var. 'Scottiae' (now known as hirsutissima), fusca, ligusticifolia, macropetala, recta, serratifolia, tangutica, verticillans, viorna, virginiana, and viticella. Dr Skinner had not been successfully flowering any large flowered cultivars but some of his hybrids of the species had survived, these included integrifolia, viticella and serratifolia. One of the Skinner cultivars 'Blue Boy', a plant very similar in habit to x eriostemon the first hybrid clematis ever raised in England in 1835, is of non-clinging habit and I believe to be the result of a cross between integrifolia and viticella. Therefore I assume that the cultivar 'Blue Boy' may be winter hardy to –40°F. At the time of writing we are flowering dark purple blue, light and pale pink forms from this hybrid which, if prove to be winter hardy, will be valuable garden plants. I have not been as generous as Dr Skinner has when I have provided its zone rating in this book, time will tell.

Of course one species C. terniflora (formerly known as C. paniculata and C. maxmowicziana) has almost naturalized itself in some regions. This species received from Russia in 1877 at the Arnold Arboretum is known as the "sweet autumn" (fall) flowering clematis and is hardy in zones 5–9.

Therefore with a little trial and error there are a range of species and small flowered cultivars that can easily be adopted to the cold harsh climate of the northern parts of the United States and cold areas of Canada.

I should now turn my attention to Mr Spingarn's comments about the large flowered cultivars for the cold north. Clematis florida and florida 'Sieboldii' introduced into North America before 1840 and forms of C. lanuginosa introduced soon afterwards caused interest in clematis but of course the introduction of C. x jackmanii in Boston in 1866 created an enormous growth of interest in the large flowered cultivars. Some of the most successful of the older cultivars and those still grown widely today include: x jackmanii, 'Henryi', 'Ramona', 'Madame Edouard André', 'Madame Baron Veillard', 'Gipsy Queen', 'Ville de Lyon' and the double white 'Duchess of Edinburgh'. These all withstood –30°F during the winter of 1933/34, without winter protection. Others which survived with some protection were reported to be 'Belle Nantaise', 'Fairy Queen', 'Lady Betty Balfour', 'Lady Caroline Neville', 'Mrs Hope', 'Nelly Moser' and the ever popular even today 'Perle d'Azur'.

Clematis viticella 'Betty Corning' is a recent introduction to North America.

Based on Mr Spingarn's old information which I value highly, and knowledge gained by other growers of these fine clematis cultivars, it is therefore easy to make recommendations for the growing of the above mentioned cultivars as well as clematis of similar habit and flowering periods. However before I deal with this I would like to record a few further cultural conditions that can be borne in mind before species or cultivar selection is made.

With a climate so variable it is difficult to make a general statement that would hold good throughout the United States and Canada. This has proved itself already with other plants such as *Ceanothus* and *Hebe* which are rarely seen grown to perfection on the eastern seaboard. *Clematis montana* and its cultivars are rarely seen performing in North America as well as they do in Europe, in some areas this is obviously due to the winter temperatures and possibly in the south due to high humidity. However, I'm sure that some of the cultivars are successful in many areas, one of the hardiest is *montana f. grandiflora* which has been known to flower without snow cover at –20°F.

Clematis viticella 'Polish Spirit' provides colourful decoration for this North American balcony in Jim McNairn's garden.

TIPS FOR GROWING CLEMATIS IN NORTH AMERICAN GARDENS

1. Buy good, strong well grown, well rooted clematis. Short, stocky well-branched plants are best.

2. Plant in the early spring so that plants become fully established by early fall and that way they will survive the hard winters.

3. Check the zone ratings before purchase.

4. Select well drained soils, or improve the soil conditions for better drainage.

5. If you grow the early, large-flowered types be prepared to lose the first flowers some springs but wait for the first crop of flowers from the new growth in early summer, all will not be lost.

6. Cover the stems and root crown with straw or other material until snowfall.

7. Carefully take down the old stems from the summer and cover them with straw until deep snow cover, this may help retain the old growth for a good crop of early summer flowers from the previous season's stems.

8. Do not always expect the clematis to reach the height as given for growing the plants under English conditions.

9. Protect your container-grown clematis over winter to retain the previous season's stems.

10. Always plant the root crown 5–7.5cm (2–3 inches) deeper than the soil level in the containers, this will build up a root crown below soil level for extra winter protection and help to prevent clematis wilt.

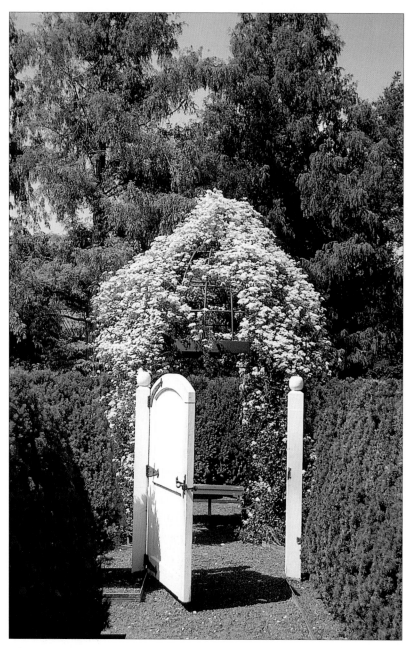

Clematis terniflora is one of the most popular species grown in American gardens.

1. Buy good, strong well grown plants. Short, stocky well-branched plants are best.

2. Plant in the fall or very early spring for early establishment.

3. Improve the soil on very dry sandy free draining soils.

4. Select native species or New Zealand and Mediterranean species.

5. Select the early spring *alpina* and *macropetala* types, the early large flowered cultivars that flower before high summer and the *viticella* cultivars that seem to enjoy the warmer climates.

6. Make sure the root crown is well shaded from the sun, be prepared to water freely in spring and early fall.

7. When planting, plant at extra depth as for those clematis for harsher climates.

8. Be prepared to have darker coloured flowers due to heat or humidity.

9. Plant pale coloured clematis out of strong sunshine.

10. Look out for some of the new large-flowered cultivars, that are similar in habit to those already growing in your area.

11. Select other varieties that come under the same sections as those already grown successfully in your garden to give a wider choice.

Gardens in the Pacific North West are fortunate and any clematis that grow successfully in England will grow most successfully here and will be quite winter hardy in Vancouver, Seattle and Portland.

Gardens in California and other states with high summer temperatures can grow the tried and tested old cultivars such as 'Ramona', *x jackmanii*, 'Ville de Lyon' as well as some of the more modern large flowered cultivars but naturally Mediterranean species such as *viticella*, *cirrhosa* and *campaniflora* will establish well. Likewise a selection of New Zealand species such as *C. paniculata*, *C. forsterii*, *C. x cartmanii* 'Joe' and some of the Chinese species such as *armandii* are ideal for Southern California and the Gulf States.

Soil is obviously as variable as the

'Ramona' is a success when planted in California, or other states with high summer temperatures.

climate and ph values should be considered but the thought that clematis will only grow in lime soils should be, I believe, forgotten. Obviously most of the species grow naturally in soils with a moderate to high degree of lime. I believe that because nearly all of the first clematis hybrids grown in gardens were grafted onto either C. *vitalba* or C. *viticella* that people wrongly assumed that these cultivars, now grown on their own roots from cuttings, should be treated as such. In woodland soils where azaleas and rhododendrons are growing, clematis can be grown quite happily. If the soil is distinctly acid then a little lime can be added during the production of clematis in containers—in our nursery the average ph is 5.5.

Clematis although requiring plenty of water during the hot spring and summer weather, also succeed better on free draining soils especially during severe winters. The large flowered cultivars, as do the species, always enjoy

and perform better when their root systems are shaded. In their natural wild habitat clematis species are found growing out from under rocks, bushes or small trees etc, which give moisture and shade to the root system. This therefore must be borne in mind when planting clematis in very hot climates.

Clematis are ideal plants for growing in containers for the patio, small town garden or deck garden and full cultural details are given on page 78–122. However in North America a few extra cultural instructions are necessary. The species or cultivar selection can be the same as for Europe, the *alpina*, *macropetala* types for the spring months and the early large flowered cultivars described in Section 4 on page 91 are the most ideal. Also included are the early large flowered double and semi-double types in Section 5. Bear in mind that the pale pinks fade more quickly than the deep blues or reds, so for the shady north facing area the pink cultivars such as

'Nelly Moser' are ideal giving lightness and colour.

The hardy *alpina* and *macropetala* types will be quite winter hardy unless the climate is severe and they can be left outside over winter (ie they will flower well if the lowest winter temperature is about 0°F, if temperatures are likely to drop lower, then some winter protection is best). The early large flowered cultivars should be protected if the lowest winter temperatures are likely to drop below about 14°F. It is very important to retain as much old growth as possible so that the maximum amount of spring flowers can be produced.

If plants are left outside with no protection the leaf axil buds (produced by fall) will be damaged reducing the amount of spring flowers. A shed or outbuilding with frost protection is required, the building should be well lit if possible and the plants can be moved inside by late fall and before the onset of winter. The plants should be slowly exposed to normal outdoor conditions in early spring before leaf development. Although this involves some work the gardener will be rewarded with an outstanding crop of spring and early summer flowers. Clematis may be a frustrating plant to some gardeners but care, attention to detail, especially watering, is all that is needed. A gardener I know, Jim Mc-Nairn in Greenwood, South Carolina only started gardening four years ago, the success he has obtained by attending to detail is outstanding. He has grown a range of twenty or more clematis in all types through trees, over fences and on his house and his success rate in establishing plants does him credit, I should add he is an ardent reader of my book!

Clematis growing in North America is very much on the increase and success rates for establishment of plants is high. Swap and exchange information with your garden centre owner, the nurseryman, with the mail order companies you buy your plants from and from fellow gardeners. I too shall be more than happy to hear from successful and unsuccessful growers in the interest of the successful cultivation of this marvellous genus.

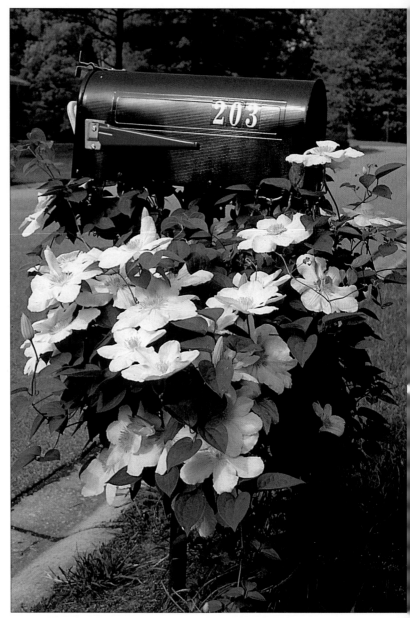

'Marie Boisselot' provides a perfect foil for this mailbox.

Clematis as a Cut Flower

Surprisingly clematis are not often used in flower arrangements but the strikingly beautiful flowers are complemented by elegant foliage and interesting seed-heads, both of which, like the flowers, can be used in many types of arrangements.

The colour range extends from pure white to deepest purple, through all the shades of blue, pink and mauve plus the creams, lemon-yellow and greens. Apart from this bounty of colour there are many forms to choose from, for instance there are both double and single large-flowered forms, the *alpinas* and some *texensis* with nodding heads, the four-tepalled *montanas* and the herbaceous clematis like the easy to condition and use C. *heracleifolia davidiana* with its strong stems and clusters of clear blue flowers. One more possibility is the sweetly scented C. *flammula* with its long strands of tiny white flowers.

Clematis can be found flowering throughout the year but, for use as a cut flower, most arrangers will rely on the outdoor season which starts in April with the *alpinas* and finishes in October with the *tangutica/tibetana* group.

The foliage of *Clematis armandii*, an evergreen clematis from China, is most handsome. The large, linear-shaped leaflets have a most unusual, strong, leather-green character. If stems of one metre are picked they are useful for pedestal arrangements when the arranger is in need of a strand of something to hang downwards. The evergreen foliage of *cirrhosa* and *cirrhosa balearica* can be also used for this same purpose. The fern-leafed clematis, as this Mediterranean species is sometimes called, is most delicate, especially the very fine cut-leafed form C. *cirrhosa balearica*. The shorter pieces of this and many other types of clematis can be used in smaller arrangements. Clematis foliage and seed-heads are especially effective in table arrangements where their form and their subtle colour can be appreciated.

When selecting a clematis flower from the garden for picking, one should choose a flower which has a thick, strong stem, not one which will bend when picked; otherwise, due to the structure of a weak stem, the flower may collapse within hours of picking. Choose a flower that has just

This formal arrangement would grace any room.

opened or, if possible, one that is three-quarters of the way open at the point when the tepals are about to expand to their full size. When an open flower is picked, beware of the condition of the centre of the flower: the stamens should be still held together and not have started to unfold toward the base of the tepals.

After selecting the perfect young flower and the stem has been cut from the plant—the length is not important—the foliage should be removed to reduce transpiration from the leaves. The stem should be placed immediately into cold water, as deeply as possible, and the flowers can then be conditioned in this cold water, if possible overnight. Depending upon the situation of the flower arrangement and the room condition, clematis flowers that I have used have been known to last for ten days; however, four to five days is the average time.

In the past, I have used clematis as cut flowers in exhibits that I have staged at the Chelsea Flower Show. The flowers were conditioned well before they were transported and

Chosen carefully the colours of the clematis can co-ordinate with the decor of your home.

arranged, and some have lasted the full five days of the show—which is indeed remarkable given the heat and conditions of an exhibit under canvas!

While using cut flowers in this way, I have grown plants especially in beds in a cold glasshouse, using a little heat to bring the flowers on and to open at the correct time. If the reader is fortunate enough to have the space available in a conservatory or cold glasshouse, growing clematis in this way for cut flowers is most rewarding. When clematis are grown in soil beds

THE MOST SUCCESSFUL CLEMATIS FOR CUT FLOWERS:

Blue (dark)
'Beauty of Worcester'
'Daniel Deronda'
'Lasurstern'
'Lord Nevill'
'Richard Pennell'
'Serenata'
'The President'
viticella 'Polish Spirit'

Mauve
'Barbara Jackman'
'Horn of Plenty'
'Kathleen Wheeler'
'King Edward VII'
'Marcel Moser'
'Proteus'
'Vyvyan Pennell'

Blue (light)
'Beauty of Richmond'
'General Sikorski'
'H.F. Young'
'Lady Caroline Nevill'
'Mrs. Cholmondeley'
'Peveril Pearl'
'Prins Hendrik'
'W. E. Gladstone'
'Will Goodwin'
'William Kennett'

White/Cream
'Edith'
'Henryi'
'Marie Boisselot'
'Miss Bateman'
'Mrs. George Jackman'

Pink
'Bees Jubilee'
'Carnaby'
'Dawn'
'Dr. Ruppel'
'Fairy Queen'
'Lincoln Star'
'Nelly Moser'

under glasshouse conditions, periods of long high temperatures should be avoided; the best clematis for picking are those which have been grown under almost outdoor conditions, but with protection from wind and rain. Clematis grown in this way will be several weeks ahead of outdoor plants. Hard pruning of all clematis grown especially for cut flowers is important, as strong new growth needs to be encouraged; and even established, early large-flowered cultivars should be pruned down to about one metre in early spring.

After many of the clematis flowers have died away they are often replaced by delightful fluffy seed heads. If the old flower head and flower stalks remain and are not trimmed off, within several weeks the pollinated seeds begin to grow. As the seed tails (styles) mature and become a silvery-grey colour, they add yet another attractive dimension to the clematis plant. As the seed heads become of interest to the flower arranger, they may be cut for immediate use or dried to preserve them for dried winter arrangements.

If you are particularly interested in growing clematis with attractive seed heads, then the early-flowering types are some of the best. The semi-hardy *C. napaulensis*, which flowers in December, has delightful large seed heads in January and February when grown under cold glasshouse conditions in England. Both the *alpina* and *macropetala* types have seed heads from late spring onwards and these look charming. As the occasional summer flowers are produced by these clematis, so one has a mix of flowers and seed heads. Most of the early large-flowered cultivars, such as 'Nelly Moser', 'Elsa Späth', and 'Daniel Deronda' have more rounded seed heads from mid summer onwards.

The later-flowering, large-flow-

The striking seed heads of Clematis fusca violacea.

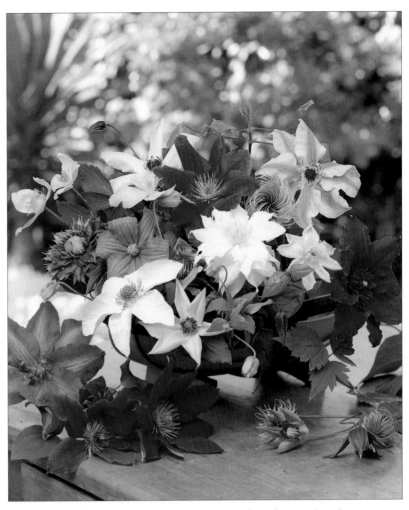

Here the clematis have been used to create an informal arrangement.

ered types, sadly do not have such attractive seed heads. So, from the large-flowered types, one must choose plants that flower before mid summer to be sure of getting this added bonus. The later-flowering species, such as *tangutica*, all of the *tibetana* types, *serratifolia* and, of course, the European native *vitalba*, are among some of the best, as is *virginiana* in the U.S.A. and *terniflora* also in the U.S.A. which is absolutely gorgeous when in full seed.

Both C. *virginiana* and C. *vitalba* have many common names; one of the best, I think, is "old man's beard" which really describes the mass of seed heads that this plant has during the late autumn months. To see a C. *vitalba* covered with seed heads, clambering over a hedgerow in England in December covered in frost on a bright morning, is a great delight.

Preserving seed heads

The most reliable clematis for this purpose are the early-flowering species and large-flowered cultivars whose seed-heads are fully developed but have not gone fluffy by late summer. Later-flowering species and cultivars are more at risk from the damp conditions which usually prevail as the season advances.

Stems can be cut when the seed-heads are in the silky stage and preserved by using glycerine. To do this, put the freshly cut stem ends in a mixture of one third glycerine and two-thirds boiling water. Stir to mix thoroughly and use while it is still very hot. The mixture should be about 5cm deep in a jam jar or similar container. The stalks and any leaves will turn a rich brown colour while the seedheads will be slightly paler and keep their silky texture. Imperfect foliage should be removed and stems should not be packed too tightly.

The jar needs to be placed in a cool but dry place, out of bright light and a check should be made on progress every few days, the mixture being topped up if necessary.

The stems are ready when the colour is even and the leaves are just slightly oily to the touch. Do not put these or dried stems in water or a damp atmosphere. Long trails of *vitalba* seedheads can be treated in this way but all seedheads must be cut before they reach the fluffy stage.

THE MOST SUCCESSFUL CLEMATIS FOR PRESERVING IN GLYCERINE:

Alpina and macropetala types
alpina 'Burford White'
alpina 'Columbine'
alpina 'Frankie'
alpina 'Helsingborg'
alpina 'Ruby'
alpina 'Willy'
macropetala 'Floralia'
macropetala 'Lagoon'
macropetala 'Markhams Pink'

Early Flowering Large Cultivars
'Barbara Dibley'
'Dawn'
'Edith'
'Gillian Blades'
'Kathleen Wheeler'
'Lasurstern'
'Lord Nevill'
'Mrs Cholmondeley'
'Moonlight'
'Nelly Moser'
'The President'
'Wada's Primrose'

Double and Semi-double Cultivars
'Daniel Deronda'
'Vyvyan Pennell'

Late Flowering species and their forms
tangutica
tangutica 'Bill MacKenzie'

Propagation

The propagation of clematis is a challenging and satisfying occupation for the keen clematis grower.

There are several ways in which clematis may be reproduced: by seed, layering, cuttings, grafting and by root crown division of the herbaceous cultivars.

Reproduction by layering

The layering of clematis is not as exciting as waiting for seedlings to flower but it is a means by which a gardener can successfully, and without much experience, increase the numbers of clematis for his own garden, or to use for swopping with other gardeners. The exchange of plants between gardening enthusiasts is always a satisfactory means of increasing one's own selection and is a way in which plants gain wider distribution.

The best time for layering clematis is during late spring or very early summer. A 15cm diameter flowerpot should be sunk into the soil near to the base of the clematis plant and within easy reach of the stem which is to be layered. The pot should contain a mixture of John Innes potting soil No. 2 and be filled to the top and lightly firmed. The selection stem should be gently bent downwards towards the pot, and the nearest node to the flowerpot should then be pinned into the soil with a piece of thick wire. Before the node is pinned down it should be split by a sharp knife—a 2.5cm cut made in an upward direction from below the node and into the node will help rooting to take place. If the cut and stem surrounding it is dusted with a rooting hormone, this will assist in faster rooting. When the stem is pinned onto the soil in the pot, an extra layer of soil can be placed over the node and a stone may also be placed over the wire pin to hold it in place.

Rooting of the stem may take several weeks and the soil in the flowerpot must not be allowed to become dry. After about nine months the layered stem will have formed a new plant; but it should be left attached to its parent until early spring, when it may be detached and the pot removed

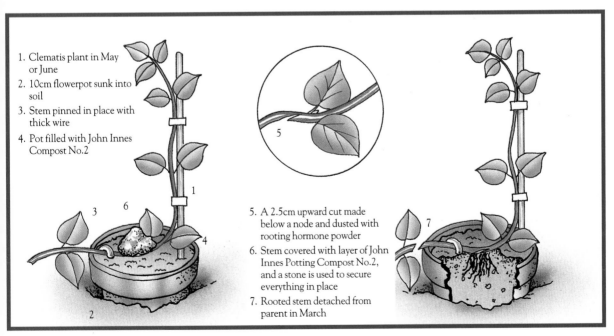

1. Clematis plant in May or June
2. 10cm flowerpot sunk into soil
3. Stem pinned in place with thick wire
4. Pot filled with John Innes Compost No.2

5. A 2.5cm upward cut made below a node and dusted with rooting hormone powder
6. Stem covered with layer of John Innes Potting Compost No.2, and a stone is used to secure everything in place
7. Rooted stem detached from parent in March

Layering

Clematis seed sown in pots, each covered with a fine layer of grit.

from the soil. The new plant should then be treated as if it were a plant purchased from a nursery and pruned as described on pages 22 to 27.

Reproduction by seed

All clematis species may be grown successfully from seed. The resultant seedlings are generally true to type, but there may be variation, either improvements or poorer forms of the plant from which the seed was collected. Obviously all clematis clones, being clones, cannot be reproduced true to type from seed. However, this does not put off the enthusiastic gardener who uses this disadvantage in the hope of raising a brand new clematis clone.

Seedlings from clematis cultivars are certainly exciting because one does not know what to expect with regard to the possible colours. Seeds collected from a blue clematis may produce white, or even pink flowers. One is, therefore, left in expectation until the flower of the seedling opens, re-

sulting in either success or disappointment. In fact, a cultivar now generally available called 'Edith', a large-white clematis with red anthers, was raised by me and was just a chance seedling from *Clematis* 'Mrs Cholmondeley', a pale blue variety.

Seed can be collected from the early-flowering clematis in early autumn as soon as it becomes brown, swollen and ripened. The gardener can judge when the seeds are ripened by the condition of the seed tails (styles). As the seeds ripen these seed tails become fluffy and are silky-grey in colour. The swollen seeds vary in size depending upon the variety and they are mostly dark brown in colour, breaking away from the old flower stalk when fully ripened.

Seeds of the later-flowering species and cultivars do not have the opportunity to become fully ripened by early autumn unless the weather is hot and sunny; therefore, the early-flowering types are the ones to experiment with first.

Seed collected during early to mid autumn may be sown in seed trays or pots immediately after collecting and removing the seed tails. Seed compost to the John Innes seed compost formula may be used and the seeds need to be covered by compost to a depth of 5mm. The container should be placed in a cold frame or glasshouse until germination takes place, which may take up to 12 months with some cultivars. During this time the top of the container should be covered with a piece of glass and brown paper and the compost must not be allowed to dry out.

As soon as germination takes place the seedlings must be given more sunlight, and as soon as they become large enough to transplant they should be potted into a 7.5cm flowerpot and grown on in a similar manner to tomatoes or other seedlings. Twelve months after germination they may be planted out into a garden position or grown on in a larger flowerpot (John Innes No. 2 potting compost) until they flower. It may take up to four

Removing unnecessary foliage.

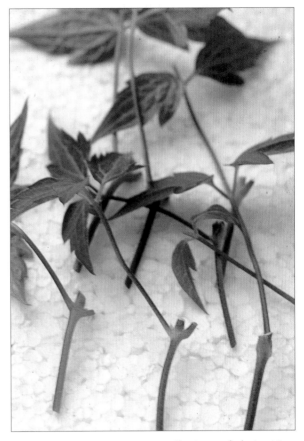

Cuttings ready for inserting.

years from collection of seed until the first mature flowers are produced. The waiting and patience is not always rewarded by a brand new cultivar worthy of commercial production and sales; but I assure you, the excitement from when the first flower bud appears until the flower opens is almost too much to bear.

Reproduction by root division

This is a simple means of increasing the herbaceous clematis and may be done as soon as the soil is frost free in the very early spring before bud break. An established plant may be dug up from its position and, by the use of two forks placed back to back the clematis can be divided. Each piece of plant detached from the original should have roots and an old stem on which new growth buds are visible. The divided plants can then be replanted immediately and given similar treatment to a new clematis planted out from a container. It is vital to keep the divided plant's small root system moist until it becomes established.

Reproduction by cuttings

This method of propagation is for the experienced gardener and the professional nurseryman. An internodal cutting is used with the cutting taken from the soft, young stems during late spring or early summer, from plants growing in an open garden position. Propagation from cuttings of the vigorous species is reasonably easy. However the large-flowered cultivars are rather more difficult. For successful rooting of cuttings a warm humid position, out of direct sunlight, is necessary.

Reproduction by grafting

Clematis reproduction by the use of grafting is now almost outdated and only used by some nurserymen, where cultivars are difficult to root from cuttings. The root stock of *Clematis vitalba* ("old man's beard") and *Clematis viticella* are the usual clematis used by professional growers if grafting is practised. If grafted plants are damaged by mice or affected by "clematis wilt", they have little chance of full recovery and this is the reason why this means of reproduction has been more or less phased out.

Pests
and
Diseases

Fortunately, clematis plants are less prone to disease or attacks by pests than many other plants, for which the clematis grower can be thankful. Like other shrubs and semi-woody plants, clematis are subject to attacks from aphid, mildew and other small pests, all of which can be easily controlled without causing harm to the clematis plant by using traditional methods.

Greenfly attacks can be easily controlled.

Clematis Wilt

The only major problem and sometimes cause of distress to the clematis and gardener is clematis wilt. The wilt is caused by a fungus, *Phoma Clematidina*, entering a damaged part of the stem. What previously has appeared to be a healthy plant suddenly collapses. Sometimes only a small part of a plant is affected but in some extreme cases the entire plant suffers. Unfortunately, little research has been carried out to find a cure and only preventative action can be taken. However, with much healthier plants being available in garden centres and nurseries, this is becoming less of a problem in gardens.

The point at which "wilt" affects the plant is generally near soil level or at least within one metre of soil level. The fungus is thought to be present in the soil previous to the attack and possibly splashed into a damaged stem which may have been twisted or cracked by wind or during cultivation. Once the fungus is positioned in its host, it grows, blocking the sap stream and causing the stem above to collapse due to lack of moisture.

If such damage should occur, all affected stems and foliage must be removed immediately and burnt. Afterwards, the affected stems can be sprayed with benlate as a possible preventative measure against further

damage. The foliage and lower stems of the plant and surrounding soil area may be treated every four weeks until the plant has recovered and produced new growth, or no further collapse by "clematis wilt" is experienced.

If a plant consistently "wilts" then it is best dug up, the soil removed from the root system and the plant submerged in a Bio Supercarb (carbendazim) solution. The treated plant can be carefully replanted in another site, and the original site should be treated again with Bio Supercarb, as a precaution against further attacks on plants replanted in the same postion. If "clematis wilt" has become a problem in a particular garden, the preventative measures described can be used to reduce the risk of future damage.

Generally only unhealthy, old or young weak plants are affected, and in most cases the clematis recovers fully within two years. New growth is produced from above or just below soil level. The important point made earlier regarding the extra depth of planting, allowing several nodes to be placed under the soil level, was intended to help the plant when damage occurs near ground level. With the extra depth of planting, new growth from the dormant buds which remain below soil level can almost be guaranteed, even after all top growth has been removed. Correct and hard pruning of clematis in the earlier years of the plant's life also helps to prevent "wilt" from being fatal and assists with a quick recovery.

Slugs and snails

These delightful little beasts can be very troublesome during early spring, eating pieces out of leaves and skimming stems of young fleshy plants. The asparagus-like shoots produced by the late-flowering species and cultivars are exactly what the slugs have been waiting patiently for all winter, so be warned! There are many slug baits and pellets available but a far cheaper preventative measure is to place a circle of spent coal ashes on the soil near to the main stems of the clematis, keeping the ashes at least 8–10cm from the stems. The coarseness of the ashes is unpleasant to the underparts of a slug or snail, and prevents them from crossing to where the young stems are growing.

Mice and rabbits

These slightly larger creatures also enjoy a supper or breakfast of clematis shoots and the mice also appear to like clematis stems for nesting material. Their control is therefore vital, though not always easy. To prevent rabbits, a collar of very fine mesh netting placed around the stem to a height of one metre usually does the trick. When mice are a big problem, a land drain placed over the clematis root systems allows the top growth to grow through the upturned pipe which will deter mice from constant attack. When the clematis stems have become strong and woody after two years or so, the pipe, if it is unsightly, may be broken and removed because the woody stems are not so attractive to mice.

Earwigs

The plants most prone to earwig damage are those growing through a densely foliaged evergreen, or on an old wall or outbuilding, where there are plenty of places for the earwigs to hide during daylight. The proprietary products available for their control can be used if damage is extensive. The damage is identified by holes in the foliage or a hole in the unopened flower bud. When a flower bud is the target, a hole is drilled through into a cavity and in some cases the stamens are removed at differing lengths.

Here are two examples of powdery mildew, the photograph on the right showing a more advanced stage.

Glossary

Listed below are 280 of the most popular and interesting clematis species and their cultivars, and these have been grouped into nine sections according to their type.

The first table is a quick alphabetical guide which shows at a glance which of the nine sections the 280 different clematis belong to.

Then each of the clematis from the nine sections are elaborated on. First you will find a brief introduction about the general habit of the plants in that section, information about pruning and more detail about the individual flower and its cultivation. The following tables within each section give details of suitable garden position and host plants.

The flowering months refer to flowering times in England. The table below can be used to convert the months to seasons.

Hardiness Zones

The hardiness zones recommended are based on experience gained by my gardener friends in the USA and Canada. These must be treated as a guideline only, as much more experience is required with the many species and cultivars that are relatively new to cultivation in these areas. Plant hardiness zones are of relevance to countries which have a wide variation in climate, particularly to the USA. These zones have been specified by the United States Department of Agriculture and are based on the average minimum temperature for each zone. The table below gives the zone rating and their equivalent temperature range. These zones indicate the areas where it is expected that the plant will perform consistently. However, it is important to remember that many climatic factors can effect the

tolerance of the plants to the site and these zones can give only a rough guide. Use your common sense when positioning your plant bearing in mind that, for example an exposed site within one zone will actually reduce the tolerance level to a lower zone than the recommended one.

Award of Garden Merit

The clematis species or cultivars which have been awarded The Royal Horticultural Society's Award of Garden Merit have been denoted in the first tables under the 'Description and Outstanding Features' column. This award is given when the plants have fulfilled all the following criteria as well as having undergone a period of assessment:

* It should be excellent for ordinary garden use (either in the open or under glass).
* It should be of good constitution.
* It should be available in the horticultural trade, or be available for propagation.
* It should not be particularly susceptible to any pest or disease.
* It should not require specialised care other than the provision of appropriate growing conditions for the type of plant concerned (eg. lime-free soil when required).
* It should not be subject to an unreasonable degree of reversion in its vegetative or floral characteristics.

January	February	March	April	May	June
Winter	Late winter	Early spring	Spring	Late spring	Early summer
July	August	September	October	November	December
Summer	Late summer	Autumn	Autumn	Late autumn	Early winter

RANGE OF AVERAGE ANNUAL MINIMUM TEMPERATURE FOR EACH ZONE

Zone 2	–50°F to –40°F	–45°C to –40°C
Zone 3	–40°F to –30°F	–40°C to –35°C
Zone 4	–30°F to –20°F	–35°C to –29°C
Zone 5	–20°F to –10°F	–29°C to –23°C
Zone 6	–10°F to 0°F	–23°C to –18°C
Zone 7	0°F to 10°F	–18°C to –12°C
Zone 8	10°F to 20°F	–12°C to –7°C
Zone 9	20°F to 30°F	–7°C to –1°C
Zone 10	30°F to 40°F	–1°C to 4°C
Zone 11	Above 40°F	Above 4°C

("s" refers to zones where southern regions only are suitable.)

VARIETY	SECTION	VARIETY	SECTION	VARIETY	SECTION
aesthusifolia	9	*chrysocoma* 'Continuity'	3	'Haku Ookan'	4
addisonii	9	*chrysocoma* hybrid	3	'Henryi'	6
afoliata	1	*cirrhosa*	1	*heracleifolia* 'Cote d'Azur'	9
'Alabast'	4	*cirrhosa balearica*	1	*heracleifolia davidiana*	9
'Allanah'	7	*cirrhosa* 'Freckles'	1	*heracleifolia* 'Mrs. Robert	
alpina 'Albifora'	2	*cirrhosa* 'Wisley Cream'	1	Brydon'	9
alpina 'Blue Dancer'	2	'Comtesse de Bouchaud'	7	*heracleifolia* 'Wyevale'	9
alpina 'Burford White'	2	*connata*	9	'Horn of Plenty'	4
alpina 'Columbine'	2	'Corona'	4	'Huldine'	9
alpina 'Constance'	2	'Countess of Lovelace'	5	*integrifolia*	9
alpina 'Foxy'	2	'Crimson King'	6	*integrifolia* 'Alba'	9
alpina 'Frances Rivis'	2	'Daniel Deronda'	5	*integrifolia* 'Olgae'	9
alpina 'Frankie'	2	'Dawn'	4	*integrifolia* 'Pangbourne Pink'	9
alpina 'Helsingborg'	2	'Dorothy Walton'	7	*integrifolia* 'Rosea'	9
alpina 'Pamela Jackman'	2	'Dr. Ruppel'	4	*x jackmanii*	7
alpina 'Pink Flamingo'	2	'Duchess of Edinburgh'	5	'Jackmanii Alba'	5
alpina 'Ruby'	2	'Duchess of Sutherland'	6	'Jackmanii Rubra'	5
alpina 'Tage Lundell'	2	*x durandii*	9	'Jackmanii Superba'	7
alpina 'White Columbine'	2	'Edith'	4	'James Mason'	4
alpina 'Willy'	2	'Edomuraski'	5	*japonica*	9
'Anna'	4	'Edouard Desfossé'	4	'Joan Picton'	4
'Anna Louise'	4	'Elsa Späth'	4	'John Huxtable'	7
'Arabella'	9	'Empress of India'	6	'John Paul II'	7
'Arctic Queen'	5	'Ernest Markham'	7	'John Warren'	4
x aromatica	9	*x eriostemon*	9	*x jouiniana* 'Praecox'	9
armandii	1	'Etoile de Malicorne'	6	'Kathleen Dunford'	5
armandii 'Apple Blossom'	1	'Etoile de Paris'	4	'Kathleen Wheeler'	4
armandii 'Jefferies'	1	'Fair Rosamond'	4	'Ken Donson'	4
'Asao'	4	'Fairy Queen'	6	'King Edward VII'	4
'Ascotiensis'	7	*x fargesioides* (syn 'Summer Snow')	9	'King George V'	4
australis	1	*finetiana*	1	'Kiri Te Kanawa'	5
'Barbara Dibley'	4	'Fireworks'	4	'Lady Betty Balfour'	7
'Barbara Jackman'	4	*flammula*	9	'Lady Caroline Nevill'	5
'Beauty of Richmond'	6	*florida* 'Alba Plena'	9	'Lady Londesborough'	4
'Beauty of Worcester'	5	*florida* 'Sieboldii'	9	'Lady Northcliffe'	4
'Bees Jubilee'	4	*forsteri*	1	'Lasurstern'	4
'Belle Nantaise'	6	'Fujimusume'	4	'Lawsoniana'	6
'Belle of Woking'	5	*fusca violacea*	9	'Lemon Chiffon'	4
'Blue Boy'	9	'General Sikorski'	6	'Liberation'	4
'Bracebridge Star'	4	*gentianioides*	1	'Lilacina Floribunda'	7
'Burma Star'	4	'Gillian Blades'	4	'Lincoln Star'	4
campaniflora	9	'Gipsy Queen'	7	'Lord Nevill'	4
campaniflora 'Lisboa'	9	*glauca akebioides*	9	'Louise Rowe'	5
'Cardinal Wyszynski'	7	'Glynderek'	5	*macropetala*	2
'Carnaby'	4	*gracilifolia*	3	*macropetala* 'Alborosea'	2
x cartmanii 'Joe'	1	*graveolens* 'Gravetye Variety'	9	*macropetala* 'Ballet Skirt'	2
'Charissima'	4	'Guernsey Cream'	4	*macropetala* 'Blue Bird'	2
chinensis	9	'H. F. Young'	4	*macropetala* 'Floralia'	2
chrysocoma	3	'Hagley Hybrid'	7	*macropetala* 'Jan Lindmark'	2

VARIETY	SECTION	VARIETY	SECTION	VARIETY	SECTION
macropetala 'Lagoon'	2	'Perle d'Azur'	7	*texensis* 'Sir Trevor Lawrence'	9
macropetala 'Maidwell Hall'	2	'Perrins Pride'	7	'The President'	4
macropetala 'Markhams Pink'	2	'Petit Faucon'	9	*thunbergi*	9
macropetala 'Pauline'	2	'Peveril Pearl'	6	*tibetana*	9
macropetala 'Rosy O'Grady'	2	'Pink Champagne'	4	*tibetana ssp vernayii*	
macropetala 'White Moth'	2	'Pink Fantasy'	7	'Ludlow & Sheriff'	9
macropetala 'White Swan'	2	*pitcheri*	9	*x triternata* 'Rubromarginata'	9
'Madame Baron Veillard'	7	*potanini* var. 'Fargesii'	9	'Twilight'	4
'Madame Edouard André'	7	'Prince Charles'	7	*uncinata*	1
'Madame Grangé'	7	'Prins Hendrik'	6	*x vedrariensis* 'Highdown'	3
'Marcel Moser'	4	'Proteus'	5	'Veronica's Choice'	5
'Margaret Hunt'	7	'Ramona'	5	'Victoria'	7
'Marie Boisselot'	6	*recta*	9	'Ville de Lyon'	7
'Masquerade'	4	*recta* 'Purpurea'	9	'Vino'	4
'Maureen'	6	*rehderiana*	9	'Violet Charm'	6
'Miss Bateman'	4	'Rhapsody'	7	*viorna*	9
'Miss Crawshay'	5	'Richard Pennell'	4	*vitalba*	9
montana 'Alexander'	3	'Rouge Cardinal'	7	*viticella*	8
montana 'Broughton Star'	3	'Royal Velvet'	4	*viticella* 'Abundance'	8
montana 'Elizabeth'	3	'Royalty'	5	*viticella* 'Alba Luxurians'	8
montana 'Freda'	3	'Ruby Glow'	4	*viticella* 'Betty Corning'	8
montana 'Gothenburg'	3	'Scartho Gem'	4	*viticella* 'Blue Belle'	8
montana f. grandiflora	3	'Sealand Gem'	4	*viticella* 'Etoile Violette'	8
montana 'Marjorie'	3	'Serenata'	6	*viticella* 'Kermesina'	8
montana 'Mayleen'	3	*serratifolia*	9	*viticella* 'Little Nell'	8
montana 'Picton's Variety'	3	'Silver Moon'	4	*viticella* 'Madame Julia	
montana 'Pink Perfection'	3	'Sir Garnet Wolseley'	4	Correvon'	8
montana rubens	3	'Snow Queen'	4	*viticella* 'Margot Koster'	8
montana 'Tetrarose'	3	*songarica*	9	*viticella* 'Minuet'	8
montana 'Vera'	3	'Souvenir de Capitaine		*viticella* 'Polish Spirit'	8
montana 'Wilsonii'	3	Thuilleaux'	4	*viticella* 'Purpurea Plena	
'Moonlight'	4	*stans*	9	Elegans'	8
'Mrs. Bush'	6	'Star of India'	7	*viticella* 'Purpurea Plena'	
'Mrs. Cholmondeley'	4	'Sugar Candy'	4	(syn. 'Mary Rose')	8
'Mrs. George Jackman'	5	'Sunset'	4	*viticella* 'Royal Velours'	8
'Mrs. Hope'	6	'Sylvia Denny'	5	*viticella* 'Sodertalje'	8
'Mrs. N. Thompson'	4	*tangutica*	9	*viticella* 'Tango'	8
'Mrs. P. B. Truax'	4	*tangutica* 'Aureolin'	9	*viticella* 'Venosa Violacea'	8
'Mrs. Spencer Castle'	5	*tangutica* 'Bill MacKenzie'	9	'Voluceau'	7
'Multi Blue'	5	*tangutica* 'Burford Variety'	9	'Vyvyan Pennell'	5
'Myojo'	4	*tangutica* 'Helios'	9	'W. E. Gladstone'	6
napaulensis	1	*terniflora*	9	'Wada's Primrose'	4
'Nelly Moser'	4	*terniflora* 'Robusta'	9	'Walter Pennell'	5
'Niobe'	4	*texensis* 'Duchess of Albany'	9	'Warsaw Nike'	4
paniculata	1	*texensis* 'Etoile Rose'	9	'Will Goodwin'	4
patens	4	*texensis* 'Gravetye Beauty'	9	'William Kennett'	4
'Percy Picton'	6	*texensis* 'Pagoda'	9		

Section 1

Evergreen and Early Flowering Species

The clematis in this section are generally only suitable for growing successfully in sheltered warm gardens in England Central and Southern Europe and warmer zones in the United States. However, they are also ideal for growing in a conservatory or glasshouse, either in containers with the less vigorous types or, if possible, direct into the soil. In cold districts, the less hardy and less vigorous species and their forms may also be grown outside in the summer on a patio for instance and taken indoors during the approach to winter. These clematis are natives of both the southern and northern hemisphere. Follow the Group One pruning instructions for all the clematis in this section.

Group One Pruning Instructions

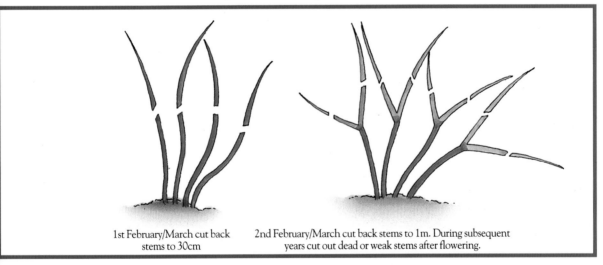

1st February/March cut back stems to 30cm

2nd February/March cut back stems to 1m. During subsequent years cut out dead or weak stems after flowering.

SPECIES OR CULTIVAR	DESCRIPTION AND OUTSTANDING FEATURES	FLOWERING MONTH IN ENGLAND (see page 78 for seasons)	HEIGHT	HARDINESS ZONE
afoliata	2mm cream nodding to open flowers. No true foliage, rush-like stems. Scented.	March-April	2.5m	8-9
armandii	5cm white open flower in clusters with large handsome leaves. Hardiest evergreen. Scented.	Late March-April	6m	6s-9
armandii 'Apple Blossom'	5cm white flowers, pink buds and stem. Large handsome foliage with attractive apple blossom-like flowers. Scented.	Late March-April	6m	6s-9
armandii 'Jefferies'	5cm white open flowers in clusters with very long pointed leaves. Occasionally flowers in summer. Scented.	Late March, April and summer	6m	6s-9

SPECIES OR CULTIVAR	DESCRIPTION AND OUTSTANDING FEATURES	FLOWERING MONTH IN ENGLAND (see page 78 for seasons)	HEIGHT	HARDINESS ZONE
australis	2cm semi-campanulate, creamy-green flowers. Ideal for the conservatory. Scented.	March-May	2m	8-9
x cartmanii 'Joe'	The abundance of 3-5cm white open flowers show up well against the coarse, fern-like, dark green foliage. Hardy to –5°C. Best on well drained soil with some protection. Ideal as a plant for the alpine house or garden room in a container. Does not cling naturally.	April	0.3m	7-9
cirrhosa	4cm bell-shaped cream flowers with red-brown blotches. Winter flowering. Scented, with attractive seed heads.	December-February	3-4m	7-9
cirrhosa balearica	4cm bell-shaped cream flowers with red-brown blotches. Very attractive cut leaf form which is bronze in winter. Scented, with seed heads. *Award of Garden Merit.*	January-March	3-4m	7-9
cirrhosa 'Freckles'	5cm bell-shaped cream-pink flowers with red blotches. Good evergreen foliage and also flowers in the summer. Scented. *Award of Garden Merit.*	October-January	4-5m	7-9
cirrhosa 'Wisley Cream'	4cm bell-shaped cream flowers which are strong growing. Scented.	January-March	3-4m	7-9
finetiana	4cm white open flowers, strongly scented, with attractive foliage.	May-June	3-4m	8-9
forsteri	2-3cm semi-campanulate creamy-green strongly scented flowers with attractive foliage.	April	2m	8-9
gentianioides	3-4cm white open star-shaped flowers. Coarse narrow evergreen leaves. Bushy habit needs dry sunny place in the garden.	March-April	0.5m	8-9
napaulensis	3cm cream flowers, nodding in clusters. Not hardy. Deciduous in August and September. Grows in October to January. Scented, with attractive seed heads.	December-January	3-4m	8-9
paniculata	4-7cm white open flowers in clusters. Very free flowering pink anthers. Ideal for a conservatory or sheltered well drained site.	March-April	2m	6-9
uncinata	2.5cm white open flowers in clusters, with attractive foliage. Scented.	June-July	3-4m	6-9

Recommended planting position for Section One Clematis

	Evergreen Trees over 15m.	Evergreen Trees over 7.5m.	Deciduous Trees up to 7.5m.	Evergreen Trees up to 7.5m.	Large Shrubs (Evergreen) up to 4.5m.	Large Shrubs (Deciduous) up to 4.5m.	Medium Shrubs up to 2.5m.	Low Spreading Shrubs & Conifers up to 1m.	Wall Trained Trees and Shrubs.	Coverage of Large Wall Areas.	Pergolas and Archways.	Climbing Roses.	Shrub Roses.	Container Culture.	Conservatory Culture.	Most suitable facing position
afoliata									✿						✿	Sheltered South
armandii									✿	✿	✿				✿	Sheltered South or West
armandii 'Apple Blossom'									✿	✿	✿				✿	Sheltered South or West
armandii 'Jefferies'									✿	✿	✿				✿	Sheltered South or West
australis									✿					✿	✿	Sheltered South or West
x cartmanii 'Joe'						✿	✿							✿	✿	Sheltered South
cirrhosa									✿	✿				✿	✿	Sheltered South or West
cirrhosa balearica									✿	✿				✿	✿	Sheltered South or West
cirrhosa 'Freckles'									✿	✿				✿	✿	Sheltered South or West
cirrhosa 'Wisley Cream'									✿	✿				✿	✿	Sheltered South or West
finetiana									✿					✿	✿	Sheltered South or West
forsteri									✿					✿	✿	Sheltered South or West
gentianioides														✿		Not Hardy
napaulensis									✿					✿	✿	Sheltered Position
paniculata									✿	✿				✿	✿	Sheltered Position
uncinata									✿					✿	✿	Sheltered Position

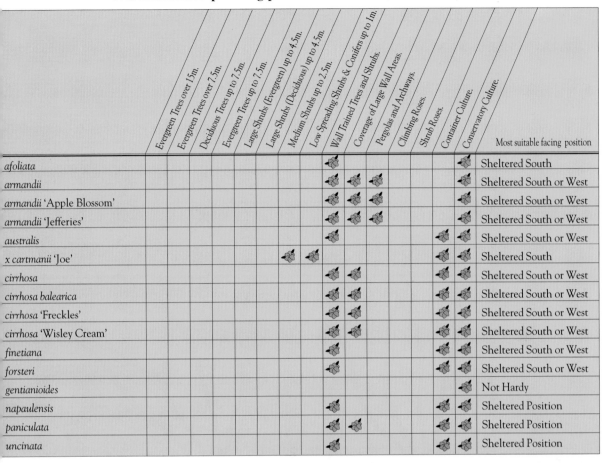

Clematis armandii is the hardiest evergreen clematis.

Clematis gentianoides is not hardy and is most suitable for the conservatory.

Section 2

Alpina and Macropetala Types

These extremely hardy and garden worthy species are natives of the European and Chinese mountains. The European species, *alpina*, has single nodding flowers with four tepals. The Chinese species, *macropetala*, has semi-double flowers which are also nodding but are slightly more open. Both species and their cultivars flower from the old previous season's stems during spring and produce occasional summer flowers which look delightful with the seed heads from the earlier flowers. This group is extremely winter hardy and ideal for cold exposed positions. Follow the Group One pruning instructions for all the clematis in this section.

Group One Pruning Instructions

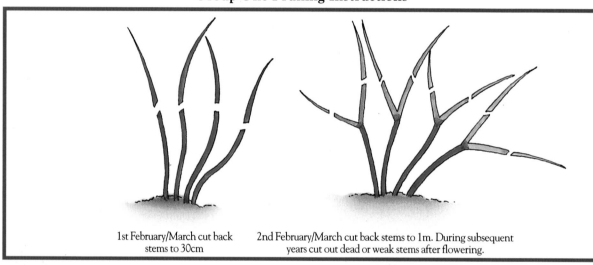

1st February/March cut back stems to 30cm

2nd February/March cut back stems to 1m. During subsequent years cut out dead or weak stems after flowering.

SPECIES OR CULTIVAR	DESCRIPTION AND OUTSTANDING FEATURES	FLOWERING MONTH IN ENGLAND (*see page 78 for seasons*)	HEIGHT	HARDINESS ZONE
alpina 'Albiflora'	White nodding flowers. 4-5 cm long. Attractive seed heads.	April-May	2.5-3m	3-9
alpina 'Blue Dancer'	Very pale blue nodding flowers 5-7cm long. Narrow twisted and pointed tepals. Attractive seed heads.	April-May	3m	3-9
alpina 'Burford White'	White nodding flowers, 4cm long with light green foliage. Attractive seed heads.	April-May	2-3m	3-9
alpina 'Columbine'	Pale blue nodding flowers. 4-5cm long. Attractive seed heads.	April-May	2-3m	3-9
alpina 'Constance'	Rich purple-pink nodding semi-double flowers, 4-6cm long. Free flowering habit. Attractive seedheads.	April-May	3m	3-9

SPECIES OR CULTIVAR	DESCRIPTION AND OUTSTANDING FEATURES	FLOWERING MONTH IN ENGLAND (see page 78 for seasons)	HEIGHT	HARDINESS ZONE
alpina 'Foxy'	Pale pink broad tepalled nodding flowers, '4-5cm long. Sport from *alpina* 'Frankie' with pretty pink inner skirt. Attractive seed heads.	April-May	3m	3-9
alpina 'Frances Rivis'	Pale blue nodding flowers, 5-6cm long. The largest form, very free flowering. Attractive seed heads. *Award of Garden Merit*.	April-May	3m	3-9
alpina 'Frankie'	Mid blue nodding flowers, 5cm long. Free flowering with pretty inner skirt to flowers. Attractive seed heads.	April-May	3m	3-9
alpina 'Helsingborg'	Deep blue/purple nodding flowers, 5cm long. A free flowering, strong coloured form. Attractive seed heads. *Award of Garden Merit*.	April-May	3m	3-9
alpina 'Pamela Jackman'	Deep blue nodding flowers, 4cm long. Attractive seed heads.	April-May	2-3m	3-9
alpina 'Pink Flamingo'	Pale pink semi-double nodding flowers with red veins. 4-5cm long. Repeat and summer flowering habit. Attractive seed heads.	April-May July-August	3m	3-9
alpina 'Ruby'	Purple pink nodding flowers, 4-5cm long. Strong growing and also flowers during the summer. Attractive seed heads.	April	3-4m	3-9
alpina 'Tage Lundell'	Dark rose purple, single nodding flowers, 4-6cm long. Unusual colour break. Attractive seed heads.	April-May	3m	3-9
alpina 'White Columbine'	White, nodding flowers, 4-5cm long. Very free flowering, pointed tepals. Attractive seed heads. *Award of Garden Merit*.	April-May	2-3m	3-9
alpina 'Willy'	Pink nodding flowers, 4-5cm long. Free flowering with some summer flowers. Attractive seed heads.	April-May	3-4m	3-9
macropetala	5cm blue, lantern-like flowers. Very free flowering. Attractive seed heads.	April-May	2.5-3.5m	3-9
macropetala 'Alborosea'	6cm pink, lantern-like flowers. Long flowered form. Attractive seed heads.	April-May	3m	3-9
macropetala 'Ballet Skirt'	6cm pale pink, lantern-like flowers. Very pretty full pink flowers. Attractive seed heads.	April-May	2.5m	3-9
macropetala 'Blue Bird'	5cm mauve-blue, lantern-like flowers. Large-flowered form. Attractive seed heads.	April-May	3m	3-9
macropetala 'Floralia'	4cm pale blue, lantern-like flowers. Pretty pale colour. Attractive seed heads.	April-May	2.5m	3-9
macropetala 'Pauline'	Very large dark blue lantern-like flowers, 4-7cm long. Long narrow blue inner tepals, one of the best of its type. Attractive seed heads.	April-May	3m	3-9

SPECIES OR CULTIVAR	DESCRIPTION AND OUTSTANDING FEATURES	FLOWERING MONTH IN ENGLAND (see page 78 for seasons)	HEIGHT	HARDINESS ZONE
macropetala 'Jan Lindmark'	4cm mauve-purple, lantern-like flowers. The first of the macropetalas to flower. Attractive seed heads.	April-May	2.5m	3-9
macropetala 'Lagoon'	4cm deep blue, lantern-like flowers. Attractive seed heads.	April-May	2-3m	3-9
macropetala 'Maidwell Hall'	4cm deep blue, lantern-like flowers. Attractive seed heads. *Award of Garden Merit.*	April-May	2.5m	3-9
macropetala 'Markhams Pink'	5cm pink, lantern-like flowers. Pretty pink form of the species. Attractive seed heads. *Award of Garden Merit.*	April-May	3m	3-9
macropetala 'Rosy O'Grady'	5cm pink-mauve, lantern-like flowers. Large-flowered form. Attractive seed heads.	April-May	3m	3-9
macropetala 'White Moth'	3-4cm white, lantern-like flowers with most attractive foliage. Later flowering form. Attractive seed heads.	Late April-May	2.5m	3-9
macropetala 'White Swan'	4-5cm white, nodding flowers. Later flowering form. Attractive seed heads.	Late April-May	3m	3-9

Clementis alpina 'Pink Flamingo' has delightful semi-double flowers.

Clematis alpina 'Blue Dancer' has narrow, twisted, pointed tepals.

Recommended planting position for Section Two Clematis

	Evergreen Trees over 15m.	Evergreen Trees over 7.5m.	Deciduous Trees up to 7.5m.	Evergreen Trees up to 7.5m.	Large Shrubs up to 7.5m.	Large Shrubs (Evergreen) up to 4.5m.	Large Shrubs (Deciduous) up to 4.5m.	Medium Shrubs up to 2.5m.	Low Spreading Shrubs & Conifers up to 1m.	Wall Trained Trees and Shrubs.	Coverage of Large Wall Areas.	Pergolas and Archways.	Climbing Roses.	Shrub Roses.	Container Culture.	Conservatory Culture.	Most suitable facing position
alpina 'Albiflora'						✓	✓	✓			✓				✓	✓	Any Position
alpina 'Blue Dancer'		˙				✓	✓	✓			✓				✓	✓	Any Position
alpina 'Burford White'						✓	✓	✓			✓				✓	✓	Any Position
alpina 'Columbine'						✓	✓	✓			✓				✓	✓	Any Position
alpina 'Constance'						✓	✓	✓			✓				✓	✓	Any Position
alpina 'Foxy'						✓	✓	✓			✓				✓	✓	Any Position
alpina 'Frances Rivis'						✓	✓	✓			✓				✓	✓	Any Position
alpina 'Frankie'						✓	✓	✓			✓				✓	✓	Any Position
alpina 'Helsingborg'						✓	✓	✓	✓		✓				✓	✓	Any Position
alpina 'Pamela Jackman'						✓	✓	✓			✓				✓	✓	Any Position
alpina 'Pink Flamingo'						✓	✓	✓			✓				✓	✓	Any Position
alpina 'Ruby'						✓		✓	✓		✓				✓		Any Position
alpina 'Tage Lundell'						✓	✓	✓			✓				✓	✓	Any Position
alpina 'White Columbine'						✓	✓	✓			✓				✓	✓	Any Position
alpina 'Willy'						✓		✓	✓		✓				✓		Any Position
macropetala						✓	✓	✓	✓		✓				✓	✓	Any Position
macropetala 'Alborosea'						✓	✓	✓			✓				✓	✓	Any Position
macropetala 'Ballet Skirt'						✓	✓	✓			✓				✓	✓	Any Position
macropetala 'Blue Bird'						✓	✓	✓			✓				✓		Any Position
macropetala 'Floralia'						✓	✓	✓			✓				✓		Any Position
macropetala 'Pauline						✓	✓	✓			✓				✓	✓	Any Position
macropetala 'Jan Lindmark'						✓	✓	✓			✓				✓	✓	Any Position
macropetala 'Lagoon'						✓	✓	✓			✓				✓	✓	Any Position
macropetala 'Maidwell Hall'						✓	✓	✓			✓				✓	✓	Any Position
macropetala 'Markhams Pink'						✓	✓	✓			✓				✓	✓	Any Position
macropetala 'Rosy O'Grady'						✓	✓	✓			✓				✓	✓	Any Position
macropetala 'White Moth'						✓	✓	✓			✓				✓	✓	Any Position
macropetala 'White Swan						✓	✓	✓			✓				✓	✓	Any Position

Section 3

Montana Types

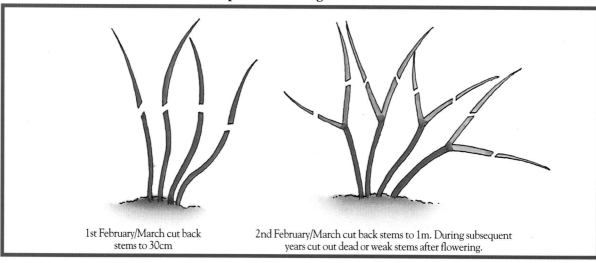

Clematis montana, a Himalayan species, and its forms, are most useful garden plants for covering unsightly walls, old buildings, etc. Their use seems endless. They can be expected to grow 6-11 metres, or even higher if conditions for growth are favourable. As well as covering walls, they also lend themselves to enhancing large evergreen trees such as straggly old pine trees and large conifers. This group flowers from the ripened previous season's stems, mainly in late spring to early summer, but also produces a few summer flowers. Follow the Group One pruning instructions for all the clematis in this section.

Group One Pruning Instructions

1st February/March cut back stems to 30cm

2nd February/March cut back stems to 1m. During subsequent years cut out dead or weak stems after flowering.

SPECIES OR CULTIVAR	DESCRIPTION AND OUTSTANDING FEATURES	FLOWERING MONTH IN ENGLAND (see page 78 for seasons)	HEIGHT	HARDINESS ZONE
chrysocoma	Pink or white forms. 4-6cm open flowers. Attractive foliage. Needs well drained soil in sheltered position.	June-August	2m	8-9
chrysocoma 'Continuity'	Pink, 5cm open flowers. Long flower stalks, good for flower arranging, flowers throughout the summer.	June-August	6m	8-9
chrysocoma hybrid	Pale pink cup shaped 4-5cm open flowers with yellow anthers. Large leaflets of a thick nature, hairy, dark green to bronze.	May-June	5m	7-9
gracilifolia	White open 'gappy' 4-5cm wide flowers with attractive foliage.	May	4m	7-9
montana 'Alexander'	White, 5-7cm open flowers. Large leaflets, with good foliage flowers best in sunny situation.	Late May-June	8m	7-9

SPECIES OR CULTIVAR	DESCRIPTION AND OUTSTANDING FEATURES	FLOWERING MONTH IN ENGLAND (see page 78 for seasons)	HEIGHT	HARDINESS ZONE
montana 'Broughton Star'	Semi-double deep creamy pink, 5cm wide, open flowers. Unusual and most attractive.	May-June	5m	7-9
montana 'Elizabeth'	Pale pink, 6cm open flowers which are beautifully scented. Award of Garden Merit.	May-June	8-10m	7-9
montana 'Freda'	Deep pink, 5cm open flowers. Bronzy foliage with deep coloured flowers. Award of Garden Merit.	May-June	8m	7-9
montana 'Gothenburg'	A full pink open flower, 4-6cm wide with prominent creamy anthers. Attractive foliage with a silver vein to the centre of each leaflet.	May-June	5m	7-9
montana f. grandiflora	White, 5-7cm open flowers. A good free flowering form. Scented. Award of Garden Merit.	May-June	10-11m	6s-9
montana 'Marjorie'	Creamy pink, 5cm semi-double flowers.	May-June	8m	7-9
montana 'Mayleen'	Satin pink, 6cm open flowers. Bronzy foliage with strongly scented flowers.	May-June	8-10m	7-9
montana 'Picton's Variety'	Deep pink, 5cm open flowers. Good bronzy foliage with some summer flowers.	May-June	5m	7-9
montana 'Pink Perfection'	Deep pink, 5cm open flowers with strong scent.	May-June	8-10m	7-9
montana rubens	Pink, 4-5cm open flowers. Award of Garden Merit.	May-June	8m	7-9
montana 'Tetrarose'	Good round, deep pink, 5-7cm open flowers with attractive foliage. Award of Garden Merit.	May-June	8m	7-9
montana 'Vera'	Deep pink, 5-7cm open flowers. A good strong growing form with large leaves. Scented.	May-June	10m	7-9
montana 'Wilsonii'	White, 5cm open flowers prominent cream stamens. Very late flowering form.	Late June-July	8m	7-9
x vedrariensis 'Highdown'	Pale pink, 4-5cm open flowers. Attractive, downy foliage.	May-June	6m	7-9

	Evergreen Trees over 15m.	Evergreen Trees over 7.5m.	Deciduous Trees up to 7.5m.	Evergreen Trees up to 7.5m.	Large Shrubs (Evergreen) up to 4.5m.	Large Shrubs (Deciduous) up to 4.5m.	Medium Shrubs up to 2.5m.	Low Spreading Shrubs up to 2.5m.	Wall Trained Trees & Conifers up to 1m.	Coverage of Large Wall Areas.	Pergolas and Archways.	Climbing Roses.	Shrub Roses.	Container Culture.	Conservatory Culture.	Most suitable facing position
chrysocoma							❀	❀		❀				❀	❀	Sheltered South
chrysocoma 'Continuity'				❀				❀	❀	❀					❀	Sheltered South or West
chrysocoma hybrid		❀	❀	❀						❀	❀					Any Position
gracilifolia		❀	❀							❀	❀					Any Position
montana 'Alexander'	❀									❀	❀					Best in Full Sun
montana 'Broughton Star'		❀	❀	❀						❀	❀					Any Position
montana 'Elizabeth'	❀							❀	❀	❀	❀					Not North Facing
montana 'Freda'	❀	❀						❀		❀	❀					Any Position
montana 'Gothenburg'		❀	❀	❀						❀	❀					Not North Facing
montana f. *grandiflora*	❀									❀	❀					Any Position
montana 'Marjorie'		❀						❀		❀	❀					Best in Full Sun
montana 'Mayleen'	❀	❀						❀	❀	❀						Any Position
montana 'Picton's Variety'		❀						❀	❀	❀						Any Position
montana 'Pink Perfection'	❀	❀								❀	❀					Any Position
montana rubens	❀	❀						❀	❀	❀						Any Position
montana 'Tetrarose'	❀	❀						❀	❀	❀						Any Position
montana 'Vera'	❀	❀						❀	❀	❀						Any Position
montana 'Wilsonii'	❀	❀							❀	❀	❀					Best in Full Sun
x vedrariensis 'Highdown'		❀						❀	❀	❀						Any Position

Clematis montana 'Wilsonii' is very late flowering.

Clematis montana 'Mayleen' has bronzy foliage and strongly scented flowers.

Section 4

Early Large-Flowered Cultivars

The clematis in this section form one of the most important groups. Their habit and flowering performance give the imaginative gardener many opportunities. Most of them will grow and flower well in any aspect and they are ideal for growing through other wall trained trees and shrubs, or free standing shrubs. They have a good range of colours, their seed heads are attractive, both flowers and seed heads make fine cut flowers. All types can be grown in containers for the patio or conservatory garden. The flowering habit of most of the clematis in this section is also long; having flowered in late spring and early summer from the stems ripened the previous season, a second crop of flowers can be enjoyed during late summer, given good cultivation. Follow the Group Two pruning instructions for all the clematis in this section.

Group Two Pruning Instructions

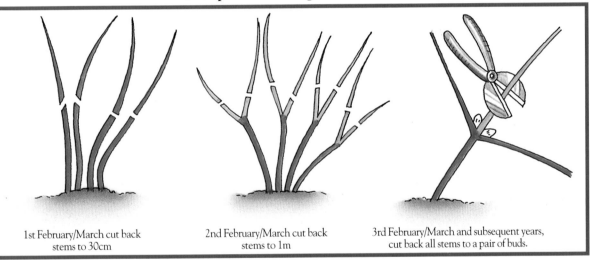

| 1st February/March cut back stems to 30cm | 2nd February/March cut back stems to 1m | 3rd February/March and subsequent years, cut back all stems to a pair of buds. |

SPECIES OR CULTIVAR	DESCRIPTION AND OUTSTANDING FEATURES	FLOWERING MONTH IN ENGLAND (see page 78 for seasons)	HEIGHT	HARDINESS ZONE
'Alabast'	Large creamy green open flowers in spring 12-15cm wide with yellow anthers. An attractive round shape, best out of full sun.	May-June, August	3m	4-9
'Anna'	Rosy pink, 15cm open flowers. Compact and free flowering in the Spring.	Late May-June, August	2.5m	4-9
'Anna Louise'	Violet, 15cm wide flowers with a contrasting red/purple bar and a striking boss of anthers both in spring and autumn. A most colourful plant ideal for a container due to its free flowering compact habit.	May, June August-September	2.5m	4-9

SPECIES OR CULTIVAR	DESCRIPTION AND OUTSTANDING FEATURES	FLOWERING MONTH IN ENGLAND (see page 78 for seasons)	HEIGHT	HARDINESS ZONE
'Asao'	Deep pink, 15cm open flowers, darker at edges. Very compact, free flowering in Spring. Ideal for a container. Attractive seed heads.	May-June, August	2.5m	4-9
'Barbara Dibley'	Petunia red, 15cm open flowers. Suitable for cut flower. Attractive seed heads.	May-June, August	2.5-3m	4-9
'Barbara Jackman'	Mauve with petunia bar, 12-15cm open flowers. Attractive yellow anthers. Suitable for cut flowers. Attractive seed heads.	May-June, August	2.5-3m	4-9
'Bees Jubilee'	Mauve pink, deeper bar. 15 cm open flowers. Very good, free flowering, container plant. Suitable as a cut flower. Attractive seed heads. *Award of Garden Merit*.	May-June, August-September	2.5-3m	4-9
'Bracebridge Star'	15cm open flowers, lavender blue, carmine bar. Attractive seed heads.	May-June, September	2.5-3m	4-9
'Burma Star'	Very deep rich blue-purple with red highlights. The fully formed flowers 12cm across have dark red anthers. Compact free flowering habit, an ideal plant for container culture.	May-June	2.5m	4-9
'Carnaby'	12cm open flowers, deep pink, darker bar. Free flowering plant, ideal for a container. Attractive seed heads.	May-June, August-September.	2.5m	4-9
'Charissima'	Cerise pink, deeper bar. 15-18cm open flower. Suitable as a cut flower. Attractive seed heads.	May-June, August	2.5m	4-9

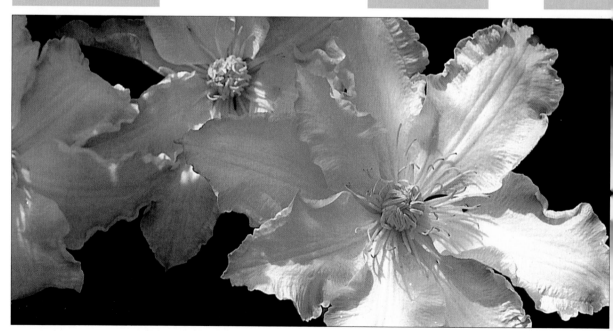

This beautiful cultivar 'Gillian Blades' holds an Award of Garden Merit.

SPECIES OR CULTIVAR	DESCRIPTION AND OUTSTANDING FEATURES	FLOWERING MONTH IN ENGLAND (see page 78 for seasons)	HEIGHT	HARDINESS ZONE
'Corona'	Light purple-pink, 12-15cm open flowers. Very compact free flowering plant. Attractive seed heads.	May-June, August	2m	4-9
'Dawn'	Pearly white/pink, 12cm open flower. Very compact free flowering plant. Suitable as a cut flower. Attractive seed heads.	May-June, August	2m	4-9
'Dr Ruppel'	Deep rose pink, darker bar, 15cm open flower. Very free flowering plant, ideal for a container. Suitable for cut flower. Attractive seed heads. *Award of Garden Merit.*	May-June, August September	2.5-3m	4-9
'Edith'	White, 12cm open flowers. Very compact plant, ideal for a container. Suitable for cut flower. Attractive seed heads. *Award of Garden Merit.*	May-June, August	2m	4-9
'Edouard Desfossé'	Pale blue, 12cm open flowers. Very compact free flowering plant, ideal for a container. Attractive seed heads.	May-June	2m	4-9
'Elsa Späth'	Mid blue, 15-18cm open flowers. Very long and free flowering plant. Suitable for cut flower. *Award of Garden Merit.*	May-September	2.5-3m	4-9
'Etoile de Paris'	Mauve blue, 15cm open flowers. Compact plant, ideal for a container. Attractive seed heads.	May-June	2m	4-9
'Fair Rosamond'	White, pink bar, 12-15cm open flowers. Compact, free flowering in Spring. Only scented large-flowered cultivar. Attractive seed heads.	May-June	2.5m	4-9
'Fireworks'	Blue-mauve, deep petunia red bar. Very showy free flowering new cultivar. Suitable as a cut flower. *Award of Garden Merit.*	May-June, August-September	3m	4-9
'Fujimusume'	Delightful powdery-blue flowers with yellow anthers. The 10cm wide flowers are produced freely on their compact plant, making it a must for a container for the patio.	May, June August-September	2.5m	4-9
'Gillian Blades'	White, 12-15cm open flowers. Beautiful shaped flower with wavy edges to tepals. Suitable as a cut flower. Attractive seed heads. *Award of Garden Merit.*	Late May-June, August	2.5m	4-9
'Guernsey Cream'	Creamy yellow, 12cm open flowers. A new cultivar. Very free flowering in Spring, compact. Ideal for a container.	May-June, August	2.5m	4-9
'Haku Ookan'	Violet blue 15 cm open flowers. Attractive flower, contrasting white anthers. Suitable as a cut flower. Attractive seed heads.	May-June, August	2.5m	4-9
'H F Young'	Wedgwood blue, 12-15cm open flowers. Very compact, free flowering plant. Ideal for a container. Attractive seed heads. *Award of Garden Merit.*	May-June, August	2.5m	4-9

SPECIES OR CULTIVAR	DESCRIPTION AND OUTSTANDING FEATURES	FLOWERING MONTH IN ENGLAND (see page 78 for seasons)	HEIGHT	HARDINESS ZONE
'Horn of Plenty'	Rosy-mauve, deep bar, 15-18cm open flowers. Very compact and free flowering, ideal for a container. Suitable for cut flower. Attractive seed heads. *Award of Garden Merit*.	May-June, August	2.5-3m	4-9
'James Mason'	A clear white fully formed flower, 10-12cm across with contrasting dark red anthers.	May, June	0.5m-3m	4-9
'Joan Picton'	Lilac with lighter bar, 12-15cm open flowers. Very compact free flowering, ideal for a container. Attractive seed heads.	May-June, September	2m	4-9
'John Warren'	Dark pink, carmine edges, 18cm open flower. Very large pointed tepals. Plant out of wind. Attractive seed heads.	May-June, August-September	2.5-3m	4-9
'Kathleen Wheeler'	Plummy purple, 18cm open flowers. Attractive golden anthers, very large flower. Best out of strong wind. Suitable as a cut flower, attractive seed heads.	May-June, August-September	2.5-3m	4-9
'Ken Donson'	Deep blue, 15 cm open flowers. Attractive flower, golden yellow anthers. Suitable as a cut flower. Ideal for a container. *Award of Garden Merit*.	May-June, August	2.5-3m	4-9
'King Edward VII'	Lilac mauve with pink bar, 15cm open flowers. Attractive old cultivar. Suitable as a cut flower. Ideal for a container.	Late May-June, August	2.5m	4-9
'King George V'	Pink with dark bar, 15cm open flowers. Sometimes produces semi-double flowers.	June-July	2.5m	4-9
'Lady Londesborough'	Pale blue, 12-15cm open flowers. Very compact, free flowering in Spring. Ideal container plant. Attractive seed heads.	May-June, August	2m	4-9
'Lady Northcliffe'	Wedgwood blue, 12cm open flowers. Very compact, free flowering plant. Ideal for a container.	June-August	2m	4-9
'Lasurstern'	Deep lavender blue, 15-18cm open flowers. Very handsome wavy margins to the tepals. Suitable as a cut flower. Attractive seed heads. *Award of Garden Merit*.	May-June, August-September	2.5-3m	4-9
'Lemon Chiffon'	A fully rounded creamy/yellow flower with a prominent yellow boss of anthers. Compact habit and attractive foliage show off the 10-12cm wide flowers.	May-June September	2.5m	4-9
'Liberation'	A 1995 introduction named to commemorate the 50th year of liberation of the Channel Islands. The deep pink tepals have a broad cerise central bar. The 15cm wide flowers have a contrasting golden yellow boss and anthers which have greyish pink filaments. Free flowering and strong growing.	May-June August-September	3m	4-9

SPECIES OR CULTIVAR	DESCRIPTION AND OUTSTANDING FEATURES	FLOWERING MONTH IN ENGLAND (see page 78 for seasons)	HEIGHT	HARDINESS ZONE
'Lincoln Star'	Raspberry pink, deeper bar, 15cm open flowers. Autumn flowers are much paler in colour. Suitable for cut flower. Attractive seed heads.	May-June, August-September	2.5-3m	4-9
'Lord Nevill'	Deep blue, 15cm open flowers. Pretty, wavy edges to the tepals, full overlapping flower. Suitable as a cut flower. Attractive seed heads. *Award of Garden Merit.*	May-June, August	2.5-3m	4-9
'Marcel Moser'	Mauve with deeper bar, 15-18cm open flower. Suitable as a cut flower. Attractive seed heads.	June-July	2.5-3m	4-9
'Masquerade'	Large 15-18cm wide mauvish blue flowers with a mauve central bar. Dark red anthers. Free flowering and compact making it a most ideal plant for a small garden or patio.	May-June August-September	3m	4-9
'Miss Bateman'	White, 12-15cm open flowers. Very compact, free flowering in Spring, ideal for a container. Suitable for cut flower. Attractive seed heads. *Award of Garden Merit.*	May-June, August-September.	2m	4-9
'Mrs Cholmondeley'	Light lavender blue, 15-18cm open flowers. Very free flowering over a long season. Suitable as a cut flower. Attractive seed heads. *Award of Garden Merit.*	May-September	2.5-3m	4-9
'Mrs N Thompson'	Bluish purple, petunia bar, 12-15cm open flowers. Very compact and free flowering in the Spring.	May-June, August	2.5m	4-9
'Mrs P B Truax'	Periwinkle blue, 12cm open flowers. Very compact, free flowering in the Spring. Ideal for a container. Attractive seed heads.	May-June, August	2m	4-9
'Moonlight'	Attractive creamy yellow, 15cm open flowers. Attractive seed heads.	May-June, August	2.5m	4-9

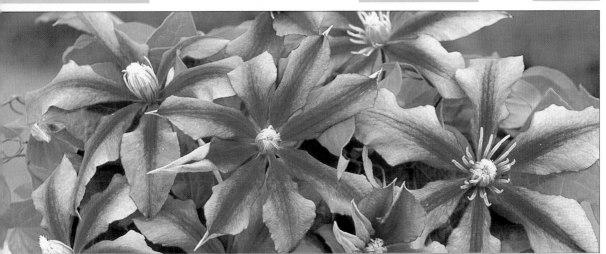

Introduced in 1995 'Liberation' is free flowering and strong growing.

SPECIES OR CULTIVAR	DESCRIPTION AND OUTSTANDING FEATURES	FLOWERING MONTH IN ENGLAND (see page 78 for seasons)	HEIGHT	HARDINESS ZONE
'Myojo'	Violet-purple 12-15cm open flowers with dark bar to each tepal. Compact habit, ideal for a container. Prominent boss of creamy anthers.	May-June, August	2.5-3m	4-9
'Nelly Moser'	Pale mauve with deep lilac central bar. 15cm open flowers. Very free flowering compact plant. Suitable as a cut flower. Attractive seed heads. *Award of Garden Merit.*	May-June, August-September	2.5-3m	4-9
'Niobe'	Deep red, 15cm open flowers. Very free flowering over a long season. Ideal for a container. Suitable as a cut flower. *Award of Garden Merit.*	May-September	2.5-3m	4-9
patens	This is a variable species with flowers of various shades of white through to blue/white, normally 10cm in diameter.	May-June	2m	4-9
'Pink Champagne' (Kakio)	Purplish pink, 15 cm open flowers. Very free flowering in Spring, compact. Ideal for a container. Attractive seed heads.	May-June, August September	2.5m	4-9
'Richard Pennell'	Rich purple blue, 15-18cm open flowers. Contrasting golden yellow anthers. Suitable as a cut flower. Attractive seed heads. *Award of Garden Merit.*	Late May-June, August	2.5-3m	4-9
'Royal Velvet'	An extremely free flowering compact plant. Ideal for growing in a container. Rich velvet purple flowers with dark red anthers, 10-15cm across.	May-September	2.5m	4-9
'Ruby Glow'	An old cultivar with a compact free flowering habit, ideal for growing in a container. Ruby rosy mauve flowers with red anthers, 15-18cm across.	May-September	2.5	4-9
'Scartho Gem'	Bright pink, deep bar, 15cm open flowers. Compact, free flowering plant. Ideal for a container.	May-June, August	2m	4-9
'Sealand Gem'	Lavender with dark pink bar, 12 cm open flowers.	June-August	3m	4-9
'Silver Moon'	Silver mauve, 15cm open flowers. Compact, free flowering plant. Ideal for a container. Suitable as a cut flower. *Award of Garden Merit.*	May-June, August	2.5m	4-9
'Sir Garnet Wolseley'	Mauve blue, 15cm open flowers. Very early flowering, compact plant, ideal for a container. Attractive seed heads.	May-June, August	2.5m	4-9
'Snow Queen'	White, 15cm open flower. Compact and free flowering. Ideal for a container. Suitable as a cut flower.	May-June, August	2.5m	4-9
'Souvenir de Capitaine Thuilleaux'	Creamy pink, deeper bar, 15cm open flowers. Very compact and free flowering in Spring, ideal for a container. Attractive seed heads.	May-June, August	2.5m	4-9

The compact habit of 'Masquerade', left and 'Snow Queen' right, makes them both ideal clematis for container growing.

SPECIES OR CULTIVAR	DESCRIPTION AND OUTSTANDING FEATURES	FLOWERING MONTH IN ENGLAND *(see page 78 for seasons)*	HEIGHT	HARDINESS ZONE
'Sugar Candy'	A new cultivar which is free flowering both in spring and late summer. Large 15-18cm flowers with pinkish mauve pointed tepals which have a darker centre bar. Contrasting yellow anthers with pinkish grey filaments.	May-September	3m	4-9
'Sunset'	A fairly new American cultivar which is long flowering, with showy 10-15cm wide red flowers, purple highlights and contrasting yellow anthers.	May-September	2.5m	4-9
'The President'	Rich purple, 15cm open flowers. Free and flowering strong plant. Suitable as a cut flower. Attractive seed heads. *Award of Garden Merit.*	May-September	3m	4-9
'Twilight'	Petunia mauve 12-15cm open flowers. Compact free flowering plant, ideal for a container.	May-June, August	2.5m	4-9

SPECIES OR CULTIVAR	DESCRIPTION AND OUTSTANDING FEATURES	FLOWERING MONTH IN ENGLAND (see page 78 for seasons)	HEIGHT	HARDINESS ZONE
'Vino'	Petunia red, 18cm open flowers. Stunning coloured flower with yellow/cream anthers. Suitable as a cut flower.	May-June, August	3m	4-9
'Wada's Primrose'	Attractive creamy yellow 15cm open flowers. Attractive seed heads.	May-June	2.5m	4-9
'Warsaw Nike'	Rich purple, 15cm open flowers. Needs a light background to show off flower colour.	Late May-September	2.5-3m	4-9
'Will Goodwin'	Pale blue, 15-18cm open flowers. Very pretty blue, long flowering season. Suitable as a cut flower. *Award of Garden Merit.*	Late May-September	3m	4-9
'William Kennet'	Lavender blue, 15-18cm open flowers. Attractive flower with overlapping tepals. Suitable as a cut flower.	Late May-June, August	3m	4-9

Plant 'Warsaw Nike' against a light background to show off flower colour

'Myojo' is violet-purple with creamy anthers.

Recommended planting position for Section Four Clematis

	Evergreen Trees over 15m.	Evergreen Trees over 7.5m.	Deciduous Trees over 7.5m.	Evergreen Trees up to 7.5m.	Large Shrubs (Evergreen) up to 7.5m.	Large Shrubs (Deciduous) up to 4.5m.	Medium Shrubs (Deciduous) up to 4.5m.	Low Spreading Shrubs up to 2.5m.	Wall Trained Trees and Shrubs & Conifers up to 1m.	Coverage of Large Wall Areas.	Pergolas and Archways.	Climbing Roses.	Shrub Roses.	Container Culture.	Conservatory Culture.	Most suitable facing position
'Alabast'				✿	✿	✿	✿	✿		✿	✿					Not North Facing
'Anna'				✿	✿	✿	✿	✿		✿				✿	✿	Any Position
'Anna Louise'				✿	✿	✿	✿	✿		✿				✿	✿	Any Position
'Asao'				✿	✿	✿	✿	✿		✿				✿	✿	Not in Full Sun
'Barbara Dibley'				✿	✿	✿	✿	✿		✿				✿	✿	Not North Facing
'Barbara Jackman'				✿	✿	✿	✿	✿		✿				✿	✿	Not in Full Sun
'Bees Jubilee'				✿	✿	✿	✿	✿		✿				✿	✿	Not in Full Sun
'Bracebridge Star'				✿	✿	✿	✿	✿		✿				✿	✿	Not in Full Sun
'Burma Star'				✿	✿	✿	✿	✿		✿				✿	✿	Any Position
'Carnaby'				✿	✿	✿	✿	✿		✿				✿	✿	Not in Full Sun
'Charissima'				✿	✿	✿	✿	✿		✿				✿	✿	Not in Full Sun
'Corona'				✿	✿	✿	✿	✿		✿				✿	✿	Any Position
'Dawn'				✿	✿	✿	✿	✿		✿				✿	✿	Not in Full Sun
'Dr Ruppel'				✿	✿	✿	✿	✿		✿				✿	✿	Not in Full Sun
'Edith'				✿	✿	✿	✿	✿		✿				✿	✿	Not North Facing
'Edouard Desfossé'				✿	✿	✿	✿	✿		✿				✿	✿	Any Position
'Elsa Späth'				✿	✿	✿	✿	✿		✿	✿			✿	✿	Any Position
'Etoile de Paris'				✿	✿	✿	✿	✿		✿				✿	✿	Any Position
'Fair Rosamond'				✿	✿	✿	✿	✿		✿				✿	✿	Not North Facing
'Fireworks'				✿	✿	✿	✿	✿		✿	✿			✿	✿	Any Position
'Fujimusume'				✿	✿	✿	✿	✿		✿	✿			✿	✿	Any Position
'Gillian Blades'				✿	✿	✿	✿	✿		✿	✿			✿	✿	Any Position
'Guernsey Cream'				✿	✿	✿	✿	✿		✿	✿			✿	✿	Not in Full Sun
'Haku Ookan'				✿	✿	✿	✿	✿		✿				✿	✿	Any Position
'H F Young'				✿	✿	✿	✿	✿		✿				✿	✿	Any Position
'Horn of Plenty'				✿	✿	✿	✿	✿		✿	✿			✿	✿	Any Position
'James Mason'				✿	✿	✿	✿	✿		✿				✿	✿	Any Position
'Joan Picton'				✿	✿	✿	✿	✿		✿				✿	✿	Any Position
'John Warren'				✿	✿	✿	✿	✿		✿	✿			✿	✿	Not in Full Sun
'Kathleen Wheeler'				✿	✿	✿	✿	✿		✿	✿			✿	✿	Any Position
'Ken Donson'				✿	✿	✿	✿	✿		✿	✿			✿	✿	Any Position
'King Edward VII'				✿	✿	✿	✿	✿		✿	✿			✿	✿	Not in Full Sun (Not North)
'King George V'				✿	✿	✿	✿	✿		✿						Not in Full Sun
'Lady Londesborough'				✿	✿	✿	✿	✿		✿				✿	✿	Not North Facing
'Lady Northcliffe'				✿	✿	✿	✿	✿		✿	✿			✿	✿	Any Position

	Evergreen Trees over 15m.	Evergreen Trees over 7.5m.	Deciduous Trees over 7.5m.	Evergreen Trees up to 7.5m.	Large Shrubs up to 7.5m.	Large Shrubs (Evergreen) up to 4.5m.	Large Shrubs (Deciduous) up to 4.5m.	Medium Shrubs up to 4.5m.	Low Spreading Shrubs up to 2.5m.	Wall Trained Trees & Conifers up to 1m.	Coverage of Large Trees and Shrubs.	Pergolas and Archways.	Climbing Roses.	Shrub Roses.	Container Culture.	Conservatory Culture.	Most suitable facing position
'Lasurstern'					✓	✓	✓	✓	✓			✓	✓		✓	✓	Any Position
'Lemon Chiffon'					✓	✓	✓	✓	✓			✓	✓		✓	✓	East or West Facing
'Liberation'					✓	✓	✓	✓	✓			✓	✓		✓	✓	Not South Facing
'Lincoln Star'					✓	✓	✓	✓	✓			✓	✓		✓	✓	Not in Full Sun
'Lord Nevill'					✓	✓	✓	✓	✓			✓	✓		✓	✓	Any Position
'Marcel Moser'					✓	✓	✓	✓	✓			✓	✓		✓	✓	Not in Full Sun
'Masquerade'					✓	✓	✓	✓	✓			✓	✓		✓	✓	Any Position
'Miss Bateman'					✓	✓	✓	✓	✓			✓			✓	✓	Any Position
'Mrs Cholmondeley'					✓	✓	✓	✓	✓			✓	✓		✓	✓	Any Position
'Mrs N Thompson'					✓	✓	✓	✓	✓			✓	✓		✓	✓	Any Position
'Mrs P B Truax'					✓	✓	✓	✓	✓			✓	✓		✓	✓	Not North Facing
'Moonlight'					✓	✓	✓	✓	✓			✓	✓		✓	✓	Not in Full Sun
'Myojo'					✓	✓	✓	✓	✓			✓			✓	✓	Any Position
'Nelly Moser'					✓	✓	✓	✓	✓			✓	✓		✓	✓	Not in Full Sun
'Niobe'					✓	✓	✓	✓	✓			✓	✓		✓	✓	Any Position
patens					✓	✓	✓	✓	✓						✓	✓	Any Position
'Pink Champagne' ('Kakio')					✓	✓	✓	✓	✓			✓	✓		✓	✓	Not in Full Sun
'Richard Pennell'					✓	✓	✓	✓	✓			✓	✓		✓	✓	Any Position
'Royal Velvet'					✓	✓	✓	✓	✓			✓			✓	✓	Any Position
'Ruby Glow'					✓	✓	✓	✓	✓			✓			✓	✓	Any Position
'Scartho Gem'					✓	✓	✓	✓	✓			✓	✓		✓	✓	Not in Full Sun
'Sealand Gem'					✓	✓	✓	✓	✓			✓	✓				Any Position
'Silver Moon'					✓	✓	✓	✓	✓			✓	✓		✓	✓	Any Position
'Sir Garnet Wolseley'					✓	✓	✓	✓	✓			✓	✓		✓	✓	Any Position
'Snow Queen'					✓	✓	✓	✓	✓			✓	✓		✓	✓	Any Position
'Souvenir de Capitaine Thuilleaux'					✓	✓	✓	✓	✓			✓			✓	✓	Not in Full Sun
'Sugar Candy'					✓	✓	✓	✓	✓			✓	✓		✓	✓	Not South Facing
'Sunset'					✓	✓	✓	✓	✓			✓	✓		✓	✓	Any Position
'The President'					✓	✓	✓	✓	✓			✓	✓		✓	✓	Any Position
'Twilight'					✓	✓	✓	✓	✓			✓	✓		✓	✓	Any Position
'Vino'					✓	✓	✓	✓	✓			✓	✓		✓	✓	Any Position
'Wada's Primrose'					✓	✓	✓	✓	✓			✓	✓		✓	✓	Not in Full Sun
'Warsaw Nike'					✓	✓	✓	✓	✓			✓	✓		✓	✓	Any Position
'Will Goodwin'					✓	✓	✓	✓	✓			✓	✓		✓	✓	Any Position
'William Kennet'					✓	✓	✓	✓	✓			✓	✓		✓	✓	Any Position

Section 5

Double and Semi-double Cultivars

The flowers produced by this group often appear rather strange when compared with the single, large-flowered types, especially when the green outer tepals are present. Sometimes, doubles such as 'Belle of Woking' and 'Duchess of Edinburgh' have several layers of green outer tepals before the true coloured tepals are present, forming a rosette-like flower. The fully double flowers are produced from the stems that became ripened the previous season. Some members of this group produce only double flowers, some, double from the old previous season's stems and then single on the current season's growth. Others produce double, semi-double and single all at the same time!

A south or west facing position is best for most cultivars, otherwise many green or unsightly coloured flowers could be produced due to lack of sunlight, especially with the first crop of flowers each spring. If you require green flowers for flower arrangements etc. then a north or east facing position will provide these for you. Due to the heavy nature of the blooms produced by this group of clematis, it is advisable to plant them to grow up through another wall trained shrub, evergreens are ideal, or free-standing low shrubs or conifers. This will avoid damage by excessive winds or heavy rainstorms when in flower. All plants from this group make ideal container grown clematis for the patio or conservatory. They are mainly early summer flowering (double and semi-double flowers) and mid to late summer (single flowers). Follow the Group Two pruning instructions for all the clematis in this section.

'Daniel Deronda' has semi-double and single flowers.

'Belle of Woking' has silvery, fully double flowers.

Group Two Pruning Instructions

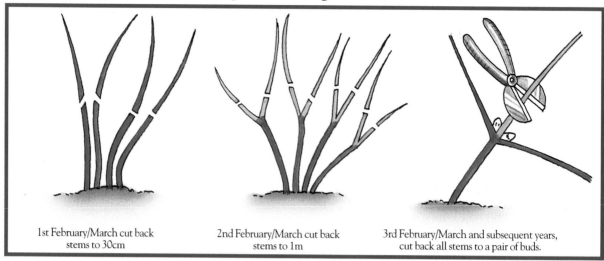

| 1st February/March cut back stems to 30cm | 2nd February/March cut back stems to 1m | 3rd February/March and subsequent years, cut back all stems to a pair of buds. |

SPECIES OR CULTIVAR	DESCRIPTION AND OUTSTANDING FEATURES	FLOWERING MONTH IN ENGLAND *(see page 78 for seasons)*	HEIGHT	HARDINESS ZONE
'Arctic Queen'	An outstanding new fully double clematis, both on old and current season's growth. The clear creamy white flowers have creamy-yellow anthers. It has the strongest habit of any double clematis and it is very free flowering. Ideal for a container for the patio garden. Flowers, 10-18cm across.	May-August	3m	4-9
'Beauty of Worcester'	Deep blue double and single open flowers, 12cm. Contrasting yellow/cream anthers. Suitable as a cut flower. Attractive seed heads.	Late May-June	2.5m	4-9
'Belle of Woking'	Silvery-mauve double open flowers, 10-12cm. Fully double flowers. Suitable as a cut flower. Attractive seed heads.	June-July	2.5m	4-9
'Countess of Lovelace'	Pale lavender blue double and single open flowers, 12cm.	Late May-June, August	2.5m	4-9
'Daniel Deronda'	Deep purple blue semi-double and single open flowers, 18cm. Very free flowering. Attractive seed heads. Good in a container. *Award of Garden Merit.*	May-June, August-September	2.5m	4-9
'Duchess of Edinburgh'	White, double open flowers, 10-12cm. Very attractive, fully double, white. Suitable as a cut flower.	Late May-August	2.5m	4-9
'Glynderek'	Deep blue double and single open flowers.	May-June, September	3m	4-9
'Jackmanii Alba'	Bluish white semi-double and single open flowers, 15cm. Strong growing plant.	June-August	3m	4-9
'Jackmanii Rubra'	Crimson semi-double and single open flowers, 12cm. Attractive old cultivar.	June-August	2.5m	4-9

SPECIES OR CULTIVAR	DESCRIPTION AND OUTSTANDING FEATURES	FLOWERING MONTH IN ENGLAND (see page 78 for seasons)	HEIGHT	HARDINESS ZONE
'Kathleen Dunford'	Rosy-purple semi-double and single open flowers, 12cm. Very pointed tepals.	June-August	2.5m	4-9
'Kiri Te Kanawa'	A startling new cultivar with a very free flowering habit both on old and new growth with fully double deep blue flowers and contrasting cream anthers. Flowers, 10-15cm across.	May-September	3m	4-9
'Lady Caroline Nevill'	Pale lavender blue semi-double and single open flowers, 15cm. Strong growing. Suitable as a cut flower.	June-August	3m	4-9
'Louise Rowe'	Pale mauve, double, semi-double and single open flowers, 12cm.	June-August	2-2.5m	4-9
'Miss Crawshay'	Rosy mauve semi-double and single open flowers, 12cm.	June-August	2.5m	4-9
'Mrs George Jackman'	White semi-double and single open flowers. Very attractively formed flower. Suitable for cut flower. Attractive seed heads. *Award of Garden Merit.*	June-August	2.5m	4-9
'Mrs Spencer Castle'	Pink semi-double and single open flowers, 15cm. Very pretty old cultivar. Suitable as a cut flower.	June-August	3m	4-9
'Multi Blue'	A free flowering compact double clematis with a spiky central tuft of narrow tepals. The outer tepals are deep blue, the inner tepals sometimes vary in colour between blue with white tips and various shades of red. A sport from 'The President' that has not become stable. Flowers 10-15cm across.	May, September	2.5m	4-9
'Proteus'	Soft mauve pink double, semi-double and single open flowers, 15cm. Free flowering old cultivar. Suitable for cut flower.	end May-August	2.5m	4-9
'Royalty'	Rich purple mauve semi-double and single open flowers, 12cm. Contrasting yellow anthers. Compact plant ideal for a container. *Award of Garden Merit.*	end May-August	2m	4-9
'Sylvia Denny'	White semi-double and single open flowers, 10-12cm. Pretty semi-double white cultivar.	June-August	3m	4-9
'Veronica's Choice'	Pale lavender and mauve, double and single open flowers, 15cm. Compact flowers, very pretty. Suitable as a cut flower.	May-June, September	2.5m	4-9
'Vyvyan Pennell'	Lilac to lavender blue, double semi-double and single open flowers, 15cm. Suitable as a cut flower. *Award of Garden Merit.*	End May-August	2.5-3m	4-9
'Walter Pennell'	Deep mauve pink, semi-double and single open flowers, 15cm. Contrasting cream anthers.	May-June, August	2.5m	4-9

Recommended planting position for Section Five Clematis

	Evergreen Trees over 15m.	Evergreen Trees over 7.5m.	Deciduous Trees up to 7.5m.	Evergreen Trees up to 7.5m.	Large Shrubs up to 7.5m.	Large Shrubs (Evergreen) up to 4.5m.	Medium Shrubs (Deciduous) up to 4.5m.	Low Spreading Shrubs up to 2.5m.	Wall Trained Trees & Conifers up to 1m.	Coverage of Large Wall Areas.	Pergolas and Archways.	Climbing Roses.	Shrub Roses.	Container Culture.	Conservatory Culture.	Most suitable facing position
'Arctic Queen'					✿	✿	✿	✿		✿				✿	✿	Not North Facing
'Beauty of Worcester'						✿	✿	✿		✿				✿	✿	Not North Facing
'Belle of Woking'						✿	✿	✿		✿				✿	✿	Not North Facing
'Countess of Lovelace'						✿	✿	✿		✿				✿	✿	Not North Facing
'Daniel Deronda'						✿	✿	✿		✿				✿	✿	Not North Facing
'Duchess of Edinburgh'						✿	✿	✿		✿				✿	✿	Not North Facing
'Glynderek'						✿	✿	✿		✿						Not North Facing
'Jackmanii Alba'						✿	✿	✿		✿	✿					Not North Facing
'Jackmanii Rubra'						✿	✿	✿		✿	✿					Not North Facing
'Kathleen Dunford'						✿	✿	✿		✿				✿	✿	Not North Facing
'Kiri Te Kanawa'						✿	✿	✿						✿	✿	Not North Facing
'Lady Caroline Nevill'						✿	✿	✿		✿	✿					Not North Facing
'Louise Rowe'						✿	✿	✿		✿				✿	✿	Not North Facing
'Miss Crawshay'						✿	✿	✿		✿	✿					Not North Facing
'Mrs George Jackman'						✿	✿	✿		✿	✿			✿	✿	Not North Facing
'Mrs Spencer Castle'						✿	✿	✿		✿	✿					Not North Facing
'Multi Blue'						✿	✿	✿		✿				✿	✿	Any Position
'Proteus'						✿	✿	✿		✿	✿			✿	✿	Not North Facing
'Royalty'						✿	✿	✿		✿	✿			✿	✿	Not North Facing
'Sylvia Denny'						✿	✿	✿		✿	✿					Not North Facing
'Veronica's Choice'						✿	✿	✿		✿	✿			✿	✿	Not North Facing
'Vyvyan Pennell'						✿	✿	✿						✿	✿	Not North Facing
'Walter Pennell'						✿	✿	✿		✿	✿			✿	✿	Not North Facing

This old cultivar 'Jackmanii Rubra' has semi-double and single, open flowers.

Section 6

Mid-Season Large-Flowered Cultivars

This group produces some of the largest flowers which can measure up to 20cm across. The flowers are not produced in great abundance at one time as with the early large-flowered and double-flowered cultivars, or the later *x jackmanii* types, but over a long period of time from early summer to Autumn, with most types in this section. Due to their more open habit, they are ideal for growing up into Rhododendrons, Magnolias, and small trees, where they can sprawl about, displaying their flowers amongst their host. Unfortunately, because of this habit they are not ideal for container culture. Follow the Group Two pruning instructions for all the clematis in this section.

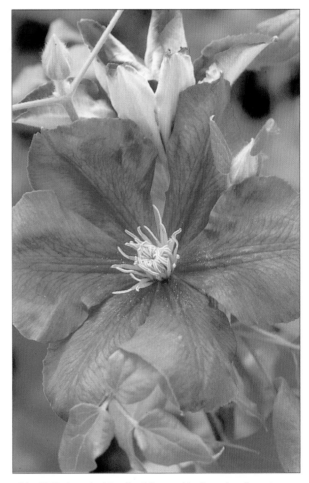

Both Clematis 'Henryi' (left) and 'General Sikorski' (right) are holders of the RHS Award of Garden Merit and both are free flowering.

Group Two Pruning Instructions

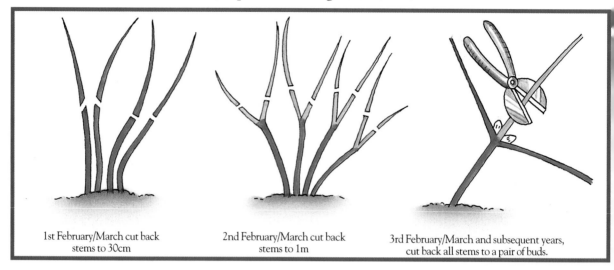

1st February/March cut back stems to 30cm

2nd February/March cut back stems to 1m

3rd February/March and subsequent years, cut back all stems to a pair of buds.

SPECIES OR CULTIVAR	DESCRIPTION AND OUTSTANDING FEATURES	FLOWERING MONTH IN ENGLAND (see page 78 for seasons)	HEIGHT	HARDINESS ZONE
'Beauty of Richmond'	Pale lavender blue with 18-20cm open flowers. Big rounded flowers. Suitable as a cut flower.	June-August	3m	4-9
'Belle Nantaise'	Lavender blue, 18-20cm big, full, open flowers. Suitable for cut flower.	June-August	3m	4-9
'Crimson King'	Crimson/red 15-18cm open flowers with contrasting brown anthers. Suitable as a cut flower.	June-September	3m	4-9
'Duchess of Sutherland'	Red/carmine 15cm open flowers with contrasting yellow anthers. Suitable as a cut flower.	June-August	3m	4-9
'Edomuraski'	A stunning deep purple blue with contrasting red anthers. The large early flowers are 15-20cm in diameter.	June August-September	3m	4-9
'Empress of India'	Rosy-creamy-red, 15-18cm open flowers. Suitable as a cut flower.	June-August	3m	4-9
'Etoile de Malicorne'	Blue with mauve bar, 15-18cm open flowers. Free flowering, good colour. Suitable as a cut flower.	June-September	3m	4-9
'Fairy Queen'	Light pink with rosy bar, 20cm open flower. Very large, early blooms. Suitable as a cut flower.	June-August	3m	4-9
'General Sikorski'	Deep blue, 15cm open flowers. Strong growing and free flowering. Suitable as a cut flower. Award of Garden Merit.	June-September	3m	4-9
'Henryi'	White, 15-20cm open flowers. Free flowering old cultivar. Suitable as a cut flower. Award of Garden Merit.	June-September	3.5m	4-9

SPECIES OR CULTIVAR	DESCRIPTION AND OUTSTANDING FEATURES	FLOWERING MONTH IN ENGLAND *(see page 78 for seasons)*	HEIGHT	HARDINESS ZONE
'Lawsoniana'	Lavender blue, 16-20cm open flowers. Long pointed tepal, large flower. Suitable as a cut flower.	June-August	3.5m	4-9
'Marie Boisselot' (syn Madame Le Coultre)	White, 15-20cm open flowers. Best large white cultivar. Suitable as a cut flower. *Award of Garden Merit.*	End May-September	3.5m	4-9
'Maureen'	Rich purple, 12-15cm open flowers. Very deep coloured flowers.	June-August	3m	4-9
'Mrs Bush'	Lavender blue, 16-20cm open flowers. Very attractive large flowers. Suitable as a cut flower.	June-August	3.5m	4-9
'Mrs Hope'	Pale blue, 15cm open flowers with dark red anthers. Suitable as a cut flower.	June-September	3.5m	4-9
'Percy Picton'	Mauve with rosy highlights, 15cm open flowers, with contrasting brown-red anthers. Suitable as a cut flower.	June-August	2.5-3m	4-9
'Peveril Pearl'	Pale lavender, 15-18cm open flowers. Needs a dark background to show off flowers to their best effect. Suitable as a cut flower.	June-September	3m	4-9
'Prins Hendrik'	Blue, 15-18cm open flower with contrasting red anthers. Suitable as a cut flower.	June-August	3m	4-9
'Ramona'	An old but reliable cultivar which prefers a sunny location to flower well. Large 12-18cm flowers, pale blue with a showy deep red centre. Large attractive leaves.	June-September	3.5m	4-9
'Serenata'	Dusky purple, slightly darker bar, 15cm open flowers with contrasting yellow anthers. Free flowering. Suitable as a cut flower.	June-September	3m	4-9
'Violet Charm'	Pale violet blue, 15-18cm open flowers with contrasting red anthers. Suitable as a cut flower.	June-September	3.5m	4-9
'W E Gladstone'	Blue, 15-18cm open flowers with dark red anthers. Reliable old cultivar. Suitable as a cut flower.	June-August	3.5m	4-9

Recommended planting position for Section Six Clematis

	Evergreen Trees over 15m.	Evergreen Trees over 7.5m.	Deciduous Trees up to 7.5m.	Evergreen Trees up to 7.5m.	Large Shrubs (Evergreen) up to 4.5m.	Large Shrubs (Deciduous) up to 4.5m.	Medium Shrubs up to 4.5m.	Low Spreading Shrubs up to 2.5m.	Wall Trained Trees & Conifers up to 1m.	Wall Trained Trees and Shrubs.	Coverage of Large Wall Areas.	Pergolas and Archways.	Climbing Roses.	Shrub Roses.	Container Culture.	Conservatory Culture.	Most suitable facing position
'Beauty of Richmond'		●	●	●	●	●	●	●		●	●	●					Any Position
'Belle Nantaise'		●	●	●	●	●	●	●		●	●	●					Any Position
'Crimson King'			●	●	●	●	●				●	●					Any Position
'Duchess of Sutherland'		●	●	●	●	●	●	●		●	●	●					Any Position
'Edomuraski'		●	●	●	●		●	●		●	●	●	●				Any Position
'Empress of India'		●	●	●	●	●	●	●		●	●	●	●				Any Position
'Etoile de Malicorne'		●	●	●	●	●	●	●		●	●	●	●				Any Position
'Fairy Queen'			●	●	●	●	●		●	●	●	●					Not in Full Sun
'General Sikorski'		●	●	●	●	●	●	●		●	●	●	●				Any Position
'Henryi'		●	●	●	●	●	●	●		●	●	●					Any Position
'Lawsoniana'		●	●	●	●	●	●	●		●	●	●					Any Position
'Marie Boisselot'		●	●	●	●	●	●		●	●	●	●					Any Position
'Maureen'			●	●	●	●	●				●	●					Any Position
'Mrs Bush'		●	●	●	●	●	●	●		●	●	●					Any Position
'Mrs Hope'		●	●	●	●	●	●	●		●	●	●					Any Position
'Percy Picton'			●	●	●	●	●				●	●					Any Position
'Peveril Pearl'		●	●	●	●	●	●	●		●	●	●					Any Position
'Prins Hendrik'		●	●	●	●	●	●	●		●	●	●					Any Position
'Ramona'		●	●	●	●		●	●		●	●	●	●				Any Position
'Serenata'		●	●	●	●	●	●	●			●	●					Any Position
'Violet Charm'		●	●	●	●	●	●	●		●	●	●					Any Position
'W E Gladstone'		●	●	●	●	●	●	●		●	●	●					Any Position

Section 7

Later Flowering Large-Flowered

The flowers produced by the clematis in this section are produced on the current season's stems. They are most useful garden plants as they can be grown over and through a great range of objects and hosts. Shrub and species roses as well as climbing roses on posts or walls can be brightened up with the flowers of these clematis. They can also be allowed to clamber about at ground level over low growing shrubs such as helianthemums or even through annual summer bedding plants. These clematis, sadly, do not lend themselves easily to be grown as plants in containers due to the habit of flowering at the end of their growing tips, which would be 2 metres in length. However with careful training of the plant this can be done. Follow the Group Three pruning instructions for all the clematis in this section.

Group Three Pruning Instructions

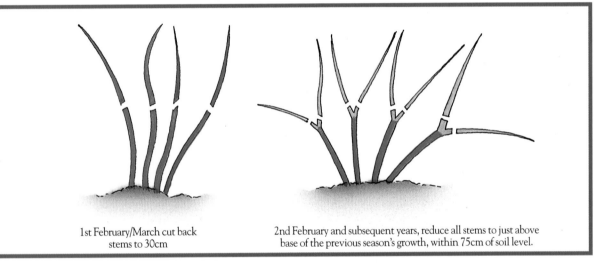

1st February/March cut back stems to 30cm

2nd February and subsequent years, reduce all stems to just above base of the previous season's growth, within 75cm of soil level.

SPECIES OR CULTIVAR	DESCRIPTION AND OUTSTANDING FEATURES	FLOWERING MONTH IN ENGLAND (see page 78 for seasons)	HEIGHT	HARDINESS ZONE
'Allanah'	Bright red, 10cm open flowers with striking blackish red anthers. Good new cultivar.	Late June-September	2.5m	3-9
'Ascotiensis'	Bright blue, 12 cm open flowers. Very free flowering. *Award of Garden Merit.*	Late June-August	3m	3-9
'Cardinal Wyszynski'	A very showy Polish cultivar with crimson red flowers and dark, almost black, anthers. Best against a light background. Flowers, 10-12cm across.	July-September	3m	3-9
'Comtesse de Bouchaud'	Bright mauve pink, 12cm open flowers. Free flowering. *Award of Garden Merit.*	July-September	3m	3-9

SPECIES OR CULTIVAR	DESCRIPTION AND OUTSTANDING FEATURES	FLOWERING MONTH IN ENGLAND (see page 78 for seasons)	HEIGHT	HARDINESS ZONE
'Dorothy Walton'	Mauve pink, 10cm open flowers. Very free flowering.	June-September	3m	3-9
'Ernest Markham'	Magenta, 10cm open flowers. Reliable old cultivar. *Award of Garden Merit*.	Late June-September	3.5-4m	3-9
'Gipsy Queen'	Velvety, violet purple, 12cm open flowers with dark red anthers. *Award of Garden Merit*.	Late June-September	3m	3-9
'Hagley Hybrid'	Rosy mauve, 10cm open flowers. Compact free flowering, late pink.	Late June-August	2.5m	3-9
x *jackmanii*	Dark velvet purple, 10cm semi-campanulate flowers. Very popular old cultivar. *Award of Garden Merit*.	July-September	3m	3-9
'Jackmanii Superba'	Rich velvet purple, 12cm open, semi-campanulate flowers. More rounded and slightly larger flowered than x *jackmanii*.	July-September	3m	3-9
'John Huxtable'	White, 10cm open flowers. Good, free flowering white.	July-August	2.5-3m	3-9
'John Paul II'	A pale whitish pink with red anthers, the early flowers are 12cm across, later summer flowers being smaller.	July-September	3.5m	3-9
'Lady Betty Balfour'	Purple blue, 15cm open flowers. Very late flowering purple which must be planted in full sun to obtain a good crop of flowers.	September-October	3.5m	3-9
'Lilacina Floribunda'	Deep rich purple, 12cm open flowers. Will also flower on old stems in early June.	Late June-September	3m	3-9
'Margaret Hunt'	Dusky mauve-pink, 10cm open flowers. Very free flowering, vigorous.	July-August	3m	3-9
'Madame Baron Veillard'	Lilac rose, 10cm open flowers. Very late flowering which should be planted in full sun to obtain a good crop of flowers.	September-October	3m	3-9
'Madame Edouard André'	Dusky red, 10 cm open flowers. Looks good in association with herbaceous plants. *Award of Garden Merit*.	July-August	2.5m	3-9
'Madame Grangé'	Dusky velvet-purple, 12cm open flowers. Lovely boat-shaped tepals. Needs a light background to show the flower off to best effect. *Award of Garden Merit*.	July-August	3m	3-9
'Perle d'Azur'	Sky blue, 8-10cm open, semi-campanulate. A beautiful coloured, free flowering cultivar. *Award of Garden Merit*.	July-September	3.5m	3-9
'Perrins Pride'	A newish American cultivar which is summer flowering but it will produce some 15cm wide flowers from the old wood. The rounded purple flowers have a greenish bronze centre.	June-September	3.5m	3-9
'Pink Fantasy'	Pale pink, darker bar, 10cm open flowers. Very pretty with brown anthers.	Late June-September	2-2.5m	3-9

SPECIES OR CULTIVAR	DESCRIPTION AND OUTSTANDING FEATURES	FLOWERING MONTH IN ENGLAND (see page 78 for seasons)	HEIGHT	HARDINESS ZONE
'Prince Charles'	Mauve blue, 8-10cm open flowers. Very compact and free flowering.	Late June-September	2m	3-9
'Rhapsody'	A very free flowering new clematis, with very stunning sapphire blue tepals which deepen in colour with age. Open creamy yellow anthers. If some old wood is left it will flower early in the summer. Flowers 10-12cm across.	June-September	3m	3-9
'Rouge Cardinal'	Velvety crimson, 10cm open flowers. Free flowering.	July-August	3m	3-9
'Star of India'	Deep purple blue, carmine bar, 10cm open flowers. Very free flowering. *Award of Garden Merit.*	July-August	3m	3-9
'Victoria'	Rosy purple, 10cm open flowers. Vigorous, free flowering.	July-August	2.5-3m	3-9
'Ville de Lyon'	Bright crimson red, 10-12cm open flowers. Contrasting yellow anthers.	July-September	3m	3-9
'Voluceau'	Petunia red, 10cm open flowers. Twisted tepals and contrasting yellow anthers.	Late June-August	3m	3-9

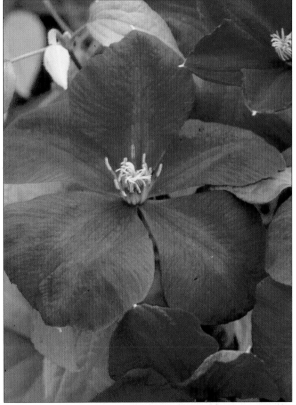

'Madame Edouard André' has gained the RHS Award of Garden Merit.

'Perrins Pride' is a newish summer flowering American cultivar.

Recommended planting position for Section Seven Clematis

	Evergreen Trees over 15m.	Evergreen Trees over 7.5m.	Deciduous Trees over 7.5m.	Deciduous Trees up to 7.5m.	Evergreen Trees up to 7.5m.	Large Shrubs (Evergreen) up to 4.5m.	Large Shrubs (Deciduous) up to 4.5m.	Medium Shrubs up to 2.5m.	Low Spreading Shrubs up to 2.5m.	Wall Trained Trees & Conifers up to 1m.	Coverage of Large Wall Areas.	Pergolas and Archways.	Climbing Roses.	Shrub Roses.	Container Culture.	Conservatory Culture.	Most suitable facing position
'Allanah'				✓	✓	✓	✓	✓			✓	✓					Any Position
'Ascotiensis'			✓	✓	✓	✓	✓	✓			✓	✓	✓				Any Position
'Cardinal Wyszynski'			✓	✓	✓	✓	✓	✓			✓	✓	✓				Any Position
'Comtesse de Bouchaud'			✓	✓	✓	✓	✓	✓			✓	✓	✓				Any Position
'Dorothy Walton'				✓	✓	✓	✓	✓			✓						Any Position
'Ernest Markham'			✓	✓	✓	✓	✓	✓	✓	✓	✓						Best in Sun
'Gipsy Queen'			✓	✓	✓	✓	✓	✓	✓		✓	✓	✓				Any Position
'Hagley Hybrid'				✓	✓	✓	✓	✓			✓	✓					Not South Facing
x jackmanii				✓	✓	✓	✓	✓	✓	✓	✓	✓	✓				Any Position
'Jackmanii Superba'				✓	✓	✓	✓	✓	✓	✓	✓	✓	✓				Any Position
'John Huxtable'				✓	✓	✓	✓	✓			✓	✓	✓				Any Position
'John Paul II'		✓	✓	✓	✓	✓	✓	✓			✓	✓	✓				Not South Facing
'Lady Betty Balfour'				✓	✓	✓	✓	✓	✓	✓	✓						Best in Full Sun
'Lilacina Floribunda'				✓	✓	✓	✓	✓	✓	✓	✓						Any Position
'Margaret Hunt'				✓	✓	✓	✓	✓			✓						Any Position
'Madame Baron Veillard'				✓	✓				✓	✓	✓						Best in Full Sun
'Madame Edouard André'				✓	✓	✓	✓	✓			✓	✓	✓				Any Position
'Madame Grangé'				✓	✓	✓	✓	✓			✓	✓	✓				Any Position
'Perle d'Azur'		✓	✓	✓	✓	✓	✓	✓	✓	✓	✓						Any Position
'Perrins Pride'		✓	✓	✓	✓	✓	✓	✓			✓	✓	✓				Any Position
'Pink Fantasy'				✓	✓	✓	✓	✓			✓	✓					Any Position
'Prince Charles'				✓	✓	✓	✓	✓			✓	✓	✓				Any Position
'Rhapsody'		✓	✓	✓	✓	✓	✓	✓			✓	✓	✓				Any Position
'Rouge Cardinal'				✓	✓	✓	✓	✓			✓	✓					Any Position
'Star of India'				✓	✓	✓	✓	✓	✓	✓	✓		✓	✓			Any Position
'Victoria'	✓			✓	✓	✓	✓	✓	✓	✓	✓	✓	✓				Any Position
'Ville de Lyon'				✓	✓			✓			✓	✓					Any Position
'Voluceau'				✓	✓	✓	✓				✓	✓					Any Position

Section 8

Viticella Types

Clematis viticella is a vigorous European species, since its introduction in the 16th century to England, it has given rise to many fine cultivars. Clematis viticella 'Purpurea Plena Elegans' is known to have also been in cultivation from about that time, although it is still not commonly grown. This group of clematis, like the large later-flowering types, offer splendid value for money, in addition, they do not suffer at all from clematis wilt. Their colour range is good and their flowering period is from mid summer until autumn. Many have semi-nodding flowers and can be grown in small trees where their flowers can be enjoyed from below, looking up into the flowers. They look equally good tumbling about through shrubs of any height, even scrambling around at ground level on low-growing ground cover plants such as winter and summer flowering heathers. Follow the Group Three pruning instructions for all the clematis in this section.

Group Three Pruning Instructions

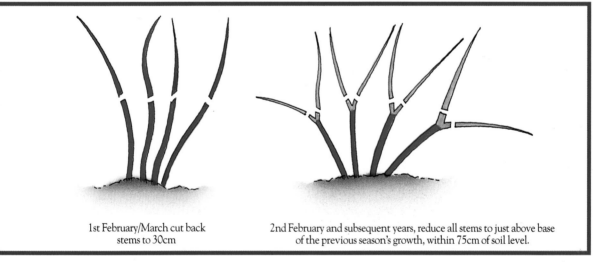

1st February/March cut back stems to 30cm

2nd February and subsequent years, reduce all stems to just above base of the previous season's growth, within 75cm of soil level.

SPECIES OR CULTIVAR	DESCRIPTION AND OUTSTANDING FEATURES	FLOWERING MONTH IN ENGLAND (see page 78 for seasons)	HEIGHT	HARDINESS ZONE
viticella	Mauve purple, 3cm nodding flowers. The species is variable, always select a good form.	July-September	3m	3-9
viticella 'Abundance'	Wine rose, 5cm semi-campanulate flowers. Free flowering.	July-September	3m	3-9
viticella 'Alba Luxurians'	Attractive flowers, white with green tips, 7cm semi-campanulate. Award of Garden Merit.	July-September	3m	3-9
viticella 'Blue Belle'	Deep violet blue, 8cm open, semi-campanulate flowers. Very large flowered cultivar.	July-September	3.5m	3-9

SPECIES OR CULTIVAR	DESCRIPTION AND OUTSTANDING FEATURES	FLOWERING MONTH IN ENGLAND (see page 78 for seasons)	HEIGHT	HARDINESS ZONE
viticella 'Betty Corning'	A charming nodding flower with four tepals of pale blue. The 5-6cm deep flowers have recurving tips to the tepals and are scented. Raised in North America.	July-September	2.5m	3-9
viticella 'Etoile Violette'	Violet purple, 7cm open flowers. Very free flowering, yellow anthers. *Award of Garden Merit.*	July-September	3-4m	3-9
viticella 'Kermesina'	Good deep red, 5-6cm open flowers.	July-September	3m	3-9
viticella 'Little Nell'	Creamy bluish-white, 5cm semi-campanulate flowers.	July-September	3m	3-9
viticella 'Madame Julia Correvon'	Red, 7cm semi-campanulate flowers. Stunning coloured flowers. *Award of Garden Merit.*	July-September	3.5m	3-9
viticella 'Margot Koster'	Pretty rosy pink, 7cm, gappy, semi-campanulate flowers.	July-August	3.5m	3-9
viticella 'Minuet'	White with mauve veins, 5cm semi-campanulate flowers. Lovely marked flowers. *Award of Garden Merit.*	July-August	3m	3-9
viticella 'Polish Spirit'	Rich purple-blue, 7cm open flowers. Outstanding new cultivar, very free flowering. Suitable for cut flower. *Award of Garden Merit.*	July-September	3-4m	3-9
viticella 'Purpurea Plena' (syn Mary Rose)	Bluish mauve, 5-6cm double, open flowers. Splendid old cultivar. Suitable as a cut flower.	July-September	3m	3-9
viticella 'Purpurea Plena Elegans'	Violet purple, double, 5-6cm nodding flowers. Delightful old cultivar, strongly recommended. Suitable as a cut flower. *Award of Garden Merit.*	July-September	3m	3-9
viticella 'Royal Velours'	Deep velvety purple, 5cm semi-campanulate flowers. Suitable for cut flower. *Award of Garden Merit.*	July-September	3m	3-9
viticella 'Sodertalje' (formerly 'Grandiflora Sanguinea')	Pinkish red, 8cm semi-campanulate flowers. Pretty, slightly gappy flowers.	July-September	3m	3-9
viticella 'Tango'	A delightful new cultivar which has a brighter colouring than 'Minuet' and is slightly redder with rounded 4cm wide flowers.	July-September	3m	3-9
viticella 'Venosa Violacea'	White with purple veins, 7cm open flowers. Free flowering, pretty cultivar. Suitable for cut flower. *Award of Garden Merit.* cultivar. Suitable as a cut flower.	July-August	2-3m	3-9

Recommended planting position for Section Eight Clematis

	Evergreen Trees over 15m.	Evergreen Trees over 7.5m.	Deciduous Trees up to 7.5m.	Evergreen Trees up to 7.5m.	Large Shrubs (Evergreen) up to 4.5m.	Large Shrubs (Deciduous) up to 4.5m.	Medium Shrubs up to 2.5m.	Low Spreading Shrubs & Conifers up to 1m.	Wall Trained Trees and Shrubs.	Coverage of Large Wall Areas.	Pergolas and Archways.	Climbing Roses.	Shrub Roses.	Container Culture.	Conservatory Culture.	Most suitable facing position
viticella		✓	✓	✓	✓	✓	✓	✓	✓	✓	✓	✓				Any Position
viticella 'Abundance'		✓	✓	✓	✓	✓	✓	✓	✓	✓	✓	✓				Any Position
viticella 'Alba Luxurians'		✓	✓	✓	✓	✓	✓	✓	✓	✓	✓	✓				Any Position
viticella 'Blue Belle'		✓	✓	✓	✓	✓			✓	✓	✓	✓				Any Position
viticella 'Betty Corning'		✓	✓	✓	✓	✓	✓		✓	✓	✓	✓	✓	✓	✓	Any Position
viticella 'Etoile Violette'		✓	✓	✓	✓	✓	✓	✓	✓	✓	✓	✓				Any Position
viticella 'Kermesina'		✓	✓	✓	✓	✓	✓	✓	✓	✓	✓	✓	✓			Any Position
viticella 'Little Nell'		✓	✓	✓	✓	✓	✓	✓	✓	✓	✓	✓				Any Position
viticella 'Madame Julia Correvon'		✓	✓	✓	✓	✓	✓	✓	✓	✓	✓	✓	✓			Any Position
viticella 'Margot Koster'		✓	✓	✓	✓	✓	✓	✓	✓	✓	✓	✓	✓			Any Position
viticella 'Minuet'		✓	✓	✓	✓	✓	✓	✓	✓	✓	✓	✓				Any Position
viticella 'Polish Spirit'		✓	✓	✓	✓	✓	✓	✓	✓	✓	✓	✓				Any Position
viticella 'Purpurea Plena'		✓	✓	✓	✓	✓	✓	✓	✓	✓	✓	✓				Any Position
viticella 'Purpurea Plena Elegans'		✓	✓	✓	✓	✓	✓	✓	✓	✓	✓	✓				Any Position
viticella 'Royal Velours'		✓	✓	✓	✓	✓	✓	✓	✓	✓	✓	✓	✓			Any Position
viticella 'Sodertalje'		✓	✓	✓	✓	✓	✓	✓	✓	✓	✓	✓				Any Position
viticella 'Tango'		✓	✓	✓	✓	✓	✓			✓	✓	✓				Any Position
viticella 'Venosa Violacea'		✓	✓	✓	✓	✓	✓	✓	✓	✓	✓	✓	✓	✓	✓	Any Position

Clematis viticella 'Alba Luxurians' (left) and viticella 'Blue Belle' (right) are both typical examples of the viticella types that love to tumble through shrubs or scramble at ground level.

Section 9

Late-Flowered Species and Their Forms

This group, which is quite variable, consists of the clematis species and their forms or cultivars which produce flowers on the current season's stems. They are basically mid to late summer or autumn flowering and can be used to enhance a large range of host plants, objects, large trees and large or small wall areas. With a few exceptions, these are all too vigorous for container culture. Details given with each plant will assist in the selection for the most suitable host. Follow the Group Three pruning instructions for all the clematis in this section.

Group Three Pruning Instructions

1st February/March cut back stems to 30cm

2nd February and subsequent years, reduce all stems to just above base of the previous season's growth, within 75cm of soil level.

Clematis thunbergii has scented flowers, but needs a sunny position.

This unusual species is Clematis viorna which has attractive seed heads.

SPECIES OR CULTIVAR	DESCRIPTION AND OUTSTANDING FEATURES	FLOWERING MONTH IN ENGLAND (see page 78 for seasons))	HEIGHT	HARDINESS ZONE
addisonii	Charming nodding pitcher shaped purple to red flowers with creamy margins to the recurved tepals, tips, glaucous foliage. Low growing habit.	July-September	0.5m	7-9
aethusifolia	Yellow, 2cm deep nodding flowers. Delightful, finely cut foliage. Scented. Attractive seed heads.	July-September	2m	6-9
'Arabella'	A non-clinging free flowering new clematis with 4-6 rosy-purple red flushed 7.5cm wide flowers, which have creamy coloured anthers.	June-late September	1.75m	6-9
x aromatica	An old cultivar with extremely strong scented flowers, which are dark violet purple, 3-4cm across and with creamy anthers.	June-September	2m	4-9
'Blue Boy'	A free flowering cultivar similar in habit to x eriostemon and non-clinging with pale blue semi-campanulate flowers, 5-7cm in diameter.	July-September	2.5m	3-9
campaniflora	White to pale blue, 3cm campanulate flowers. Pretty Portuguese species.	July-August	4.5m	6-9
campaniflora 'Lisboa'	Its mauve-bluish 4cm wide flowers are most attractive and abundant.	June-September	4.5m	6-9
connata	A late flowering species with creamy yellow bell-like flowers with recurved tips to the four tepals and attractive foliage. Flowers 3-4cm long.	Mid September-mid October	5m	6-9
chinensis	A good autumn flowering species with scented white flowers, 3-4cm across. Needs a sunny situation to flower well.	September	5m	8-9
x durandii	Deep indigo-blue, 8cm semi-campanulate flowers. Non-clinging habit. Good for cut flowers. Award of Garden Merit.	July-September	1.5m	5-9
x eriostemon	Purple blue, 5-6cm semi-campanulate flowers. Non-clinging habit.	July-September	2m	3-9
x fargesioides (syn 'Summer Snow')	White, 4cm open flowers. Very free flowering, vigorous new cultivar. Attractive seed heads.	July-September	6m	3-9
flammula	White, 2cm star-like flowers. Very free flowering and scented. Attractive seed heads.	July-September	4-5m	6-9
florida 'Alba Plena'	White, double 8cm open flower. Needs a sheltered site, free flowering. Suitable as a cut flower.	June-September	2.3m	6-9
florida 'Sieboldii' (syn Bicolour)	White, purple centre, 8cm open flowers. Needs a sheltered site, very free flowering. Suitable as a cut flower.	June-September	2-3m	6-9

SPECIES OR CULTIVAR	DESCRIPTION AND OUTSTANDING FEATURES	FLOWERING MONTH IN ENGLAND (see page 78 for seasons)	HEIGHT	HARDINESS ZONE
fusca violacea	Purple, 3cm deep nodding flowers. Unusual hairy bell flower. Outstanding seed heads.	July-August	2m	5-9
glauca akebioides	Yellow, 3cm nodding flowers. Very attractive foliage. Attractive seed heads.	July-September	5-6m	4-9
graveolens 'Gravetye Variety'	Yellow, 4cm wide lantern-like flowers. Attractive green foliage. Not as vigorous as other in this *orientalis* group. Seed heads suitable for cutting.	July-September	4m	4-9
heracleifolia 'Côte d'Azur'	Blue, 2cm bell flowers, in clusters. Herbaceous (sub Shrub). Suitable for cut flower. Attractive seed heads. Scented.	July-August	.75m	5-9
heracleifolia davidiana	Blue, 2cm flowers in clusters. Herbaceous plant. Suitable as a cut flower, attractive seed heads. Scented.	July-September	.90m	5-9
heracleifolia 'Mrs Robert Brydon'	Bluish white, 2cm cluster flowers. Sub-shrub habit, very free flowering. Suitable as a cut flower.	July-September	2m	5-9
heracleifolia 'Wyevale'	Pale blue, 2cm cluster flowers. Herbaceous plant. Suitable as a cut flower, attractive seed heads. Scented.	July-September	.90m	5-9
'Huldine'	White, 8cm open flowers, strong growing cultivar. Suitable as a cut flower.	July-September	5-6m	4-9
integrifolia	Dark blue, 5cm long, bell flowers. Herbaceous plant, free flowering. Suitable as a cut flower, attractive seed heads. Scented.	July-August	.75m	4-9
integrifolia 'Alba'	White, 5cm long, bell flowers. Herbaceous plant, good scent. Suitable as a cut flower. Attractive seed heads.	July-August	.75m	4-9
integrifolia 'Olgae'	Pale blue, 4cm long, bell flowers. Herbaceous plant, good pale blue. Suitable as a cut flower. Attractive seed heads. Scented.	July-September	.75m	4-9
integrifolia 'Pangbourne Pink'	A stunning beautiful deep reddish pink form of the species, which is most free flowering.	June-September	.75cm	4-9
integrifolia 'Rosea'	Pink, 5cm long, bell flowers. Herbaceous plant, pretty pink. Suitable as a cut flower. Attractive seed heads. Scented.	July-August	.75m	4-9
japonica	Brownish-red, 3cm, deep nodding flowers. Attractive thick tepalled flowers.	Late May-June	2m	6-9
x jouiniana 'Praecox'	Off white, bluish 3cm cluster flowers. Free flowering. Best used as a ground cover plant. *Award of Garden Merit.*	July-September	2m	3-9

SPECIES OR CULTIVAR	DESCRIPTION AND OUTSTANDING FEATURES	FLOWERING MONTH IN ENGLAND (see page 78 for seasons)	HEIGHT	HARDINESS ZONE
'Petit Faucon'	A stunning new non-clinging cultivar with bronze green new foliage. A most free flowering compact plant for the mixed border. The intense deep blue four tepalled flowers reveal an orange, yellow centre as they age.	June-September	1m	4-9
pitcherii	Purple, 3-4cm deep, nodding flowers. Beautiful pitcher-shaped flowers. Suitable as a cut flower. Attractive seed heads.	July-September	3m	5-9
potanini var 'Fargesii'	White, 4cm open flowers. Free flowering, silky seed heads.	July-September	5m	3-9
recta	White, 2cm wide, starry flowers. Herbaceous plant, strong scent. Attractive seed heads.	July-September	1-1.5m	3-9
recta 'Purpurea'	White, 2cm wide, starry flowers. Purple foliage, herbaceous plant. Attractive seed heads. Scented.	July-September	1-1.5m	3-9
rehderiana	Yellow, 2cm deep, bell flowers in clusters. Scented, cowslip-like flowers. Attractive seed heads. Award of Garden Merit.	September-October	5-6m	7-9
serratifolia	Yellow, 3cm wide, nodding flowers. Attractive seed heads. A good plant for ground cover.	July-September	5-6m	3-9
songarica	White, 2cm wide, starry flowers. Attractive grey foliage. Masses of tiny white flowers with red anthers. Seed heads.	July-September	1.5m	7-9
stans	Pale blue, 2cm flowers, in clusters. Herbaceous plant. Suitable as a cut flower. Attractive seed heads.	July-August	.75m	4-9
tangutica	Yellow, 3cm wide, nodding flowers. Very attractive seed heads suitable for cutting. Free flowering.	July-September	5-6m	4-9
tangutica 'Aureolin'	Yellow, 5cm deep, bell flowers. Masses of flowers. Pretty seed heads which are suitable for cutting. Award of Garden Merit.	June-September	4-5m	4-9
tangutica 'Bill Mackenzie'	Yellow, 4cm long, nodding bell flowers. Vigorous and free flowering. Attractive seed heads suitable for cutting. Award of Garden Merit.	July-October/November	6m	4-9
tangutica 'Burford Variety'	Yellow, 4cm long, nodding bell flowers. Thick tepals, vigorous. Attractive seeds heads, suitable for cutting.	July-November	6m	4-9
tangutica 'Helios'	A compact new cultivar which is ideal for small gardens, the lantern-like yellow tepalled flowers open as they mature. Attractive seed heads. Flowers 4-6cm across.	June-September	1-2m	4-9

SPECIES OR CULTIVAR	DESCRIPTION AND OUTSTANDING FEATURES	FLOWERING MONTH IN ENGLAND (see page 78 for seasons)	HEIGHT	HARDINESS ZONE
terniflora	White, 2cm flowers, in panicles. Flowers best in full sun. Attractive seed heads. Scented.	August-October	6m	5-9
terniflora 'Robusta'	A large leaved form of the species which is sometimes nearly evergreen and has a silver stripe to the centre of the leaflets. Masses of hawthorn scented 5cm wide four tepalled flowers. Needs a sunny situation to flower well.	August-September	7m	5-9
texensis 'Duchess of Albany'	Pink, 5cm upright, tulip-like flowers. Very pretty flower, free flowering. Suitable as a cut flower. Attractive seed heads. *Award of Garden Merit.*	July-September	3m	3-9
texensis 'Etoile Rose'	Deep pink, 4cm deep, nodding flowers. Very free flowering. Suitable as a cut flower.	July-September	2.5m	4-9
texensis 'Gravetye Beauty'	Stunning cherry-red, 5cm upright open tulip-like flowers. Suitable as a cut flower.	July-September	3m	4-9
texensis 'Pagoda'	Pink mauve, 4cm deep, pretty nodding flowers. Suitable for cut flower.	July-September	2m	4-9
texensis 'Sir Trevor Lawrence'	Bright bluish-crimson, 5cm upright tulip-like flowers. Very colourful form. Suitable for cut flower.	July-September	3m	4-9
thunbergii	White, 3cm star-like flowers. Needs a sunny position, nicely scented flowers.	August-September	4m	8-9
tibetana	Yellow, 3cm deep, bell flowers. Attractive grey foliage and pretty seed heads.	July-September	5m	5-9
tibetana ssp. vernayi 'Ludlow and Sherriff'	Yellow, 4cm open nodding flowers. Attractive foliage, thick tepals. Attractive seed heads. *Award of Garden Merit.*	July-September	4.5m	5-9
x triternata 'Rubromarginata'	2cm starry open flowers with white tepals with reddish pink margins, produced in clusters. Very strongly scented. *Award of Garden Merit.*	July-September	5m	5-9
viorna	Creamy pink-red, 3-4cm long, pitcher-shaped flowers. This unusual species has attractive seedheads.	July-August	2m	4-9
vitalba	White, cream 2cm starry flowers, in clusters. 'Old Man's Beard'. Best grown for its lovely seed heads which are suitable for cutting. Scented.	July-September	9m	4-9

Recommended planting position for Section Nine Clematis

	Evergreen Trees over 15m.	Evergreen Trees over 7.5m.	Deciduous Trees up to 7.5m.	Evergreen Trees up to 7.5m.	Large Shrubs (Evergreen) up to 4.5m.	Large Shrubs (Deciduous) up to 4.5m.	Medium Shrubs up to 4.5m.	Low Spreading Shrubs up to 2.5m.	Wall Trained Trees & Conifers up to 1m.	Coverage of Large Wall Areas.	Pergolas and Archways.	Climbing Roses.	Shrub Roses.	Container Culture.	Conservatory Culture.	Most suitable facing position
addisonii						✓		✓				✓				Best in Sun
aethusifolia						✓	✓	✓		✓	✓			✓	✓	Any Position
'Arabella'				✓	✓	✓	✓	✓		✓	✓	✓				Any Position
x aromatica				✓	✓	✓	✓	✓		✓	✓	✓				Any Position
'Blue Boy'					✓	✓	✓	✓		✓	✓					Any Position
campaniflora		✓	✓	✓	✓	✓	✓	✓		✓	✓					Any Position
campaniflora 'Lisboa'		✓	✓	✓	✓	✓	✓	✓		✓	✓					Any Position
connata		✓	✓	✓					✓	✓						Best in Full Sun
chinensis		✓	✓	✓					✓	✓	✓					Best in Full Sun
x durandii						✓	✓	✓			✓				✓	Any Position
x eriostemon				✓	✓	✓	✓	✓		✓	✓					Any Position
x fargesioides (syn 'Summer Snow')	✓	✓	✓						✓	✓	✓					Any Position
flammula	✓	✓	✓						✓	✓	✓					Any Position
florida 'Alba Plena'				✓	✓	✓	✓	✓					✓	✓		South or West Facing
florida 'Sieboldii'				✓	✓	✓	✓	✓					✓	✓		South or West Facing
fusca violacea						✓	✓	✓								Any Position
glauca akebioides		✓	✓						✓	✓						Any Position
graveolens 'Gravetye Variety'		✓	✓	✓					✓	✓						Any Position
heracleifolia 'Côte d'Azur'						Herbaceous Clematis										Any Position
heracleifolia davidiana						Herbaceous Clematis										Any Position
heracleifolia 'Mrs Robert Brydon'								✓	✓	✓						Any Position
heracleifolia 'Wyevale'						Herbaceous Clematis										Any Position
'Huldine'	✓	✓	✓						✓	✓	✓					Any Position
integrifolia								✓								Any Position, Herbaceous
integrifolia 'Alba'								✓								Any Position, Herbaceous
integrifolia 'Olgae'								✓								Any Position, Herbaceous
integrifolia 'Pangbourne Pink'								✓								Any Position, Herbaceous
integrifolia 'Rosea'								✓								Any Position, Herbaceous
japonica						✓	✓	✓								Any Position
x jouiniana 'Praecox'								✓		✓	✓					Any Position
'Petit Faucon'				✓	✓	✓	✓	✓		✓	✓	✓	✓	✓		Any Position
pitcherii				✓	✓	✓	✓	✓								Any Position
potanini var 'Fargesii'		✓	✓						✓	✓	✓					Any Position
recta						Herbaceous Clematis										Any Position
recta 'Purpurea'						Herbaceous Clematis										Any Position

	Evergreen Trees over 15m.	Evergreen Trees over 7.5m.	Deciduous Trees up to 7.5m.	Evergreen Trees up to 7.5m.	Large Shrubs (Evergreen) up to 4.5m.	Large Shrubs (Deciduous) up to 4.5m.	Medium Shrubs up to 2.5m.	Low Spreading Shrubs up to 2.5m.	Wall Trained Trees & Conifers up to 1m.	Coverage of Large Wall Areas.	Pergolas and Archways.	Climbing Roses.	Shrub Roses.	Container Culture.	Conservatory Culture.	Most suitable facing position
rehderiana		✓	✓	✓						✓	✓					Any Position
serratifolia		✓	✓							✓	✓					Any Position
songarica					✓	✓	✓	✓								Any Position
stans	Herbaceous Clematis															Any Position
tangutica		✓	✓							✓	✓					Any Position
tangutica 'Aureolin'		✓	✓							✓	✓					Any Position
tangutica 'Bill MacKenzie'	✓	✓	✓							✓	✓					Any Position
tangutica 'Burford Variety'	✓	✓	✓							✓	✓					Any Position
tangutica 'Helios'		✓	✓	✓	✓				✓		✓					Any Position
terniflora	✓	✓	✓							✓	✓					Best in Sun
ternifilora 'Robusta'		✓	✓	✓	✓				✓	✓						Best in Full Sun
texensis 'Duchess of Albany'					✓	✓	✓	✓	✓	✓	✓	✓	✓			Any Position
texensis 'Etoile Rose'					✓	✓	✓	✓			✓	✓	✓			Any Position
texensis 'Gravetye Beauty'					✓	✓	✓	✓	✓	✓	✓	✓	✓			Any Position
texensis 'Pagoda'					✓	✓	✓	✓	✓			✓	✓			Any Position
texensis 'Sir Trevor Lawrence'					✓	✓	✓	✓	✓			✓	✓			Any Position
thunbergii		✓	✓		✓					✓	✓					Sheltered, in Full Sun
tibetana		✓	✓							✓	✓					Any Position
tibetana ssp. vernayi 'L&S'		✓	✓	✓				✓		✓	✓					Any Position
x triternata 'Rubromarginata'	✓	✓	✓							✓	✓					Any Position
viorna					✓	✓	✓	✓	✓							Any Position
vitalba	✓									✓	✓					Any Position

Clematis campaniflora heralds from Portugal.

Clematis integrifolia 'Alba' is a herbaceous plant with good scent.

Index